THE WEALTH BUILDER CHALLENGE

THE WEALTH BUILDER CHALLENGE

Ricky Grunden, Sr. and Dave Ragan

Copyright © 2017 by Ricky Grunden, Sr. and Dave Ragan

All rights reserved. No part of this book may be reproduced or transmitted in any form or by any means, electronic or mechanical, including photocopying, recording, or by any information storage and retrieval system, except in the case of brief quotations embodied in critical articles and reviews, without prior written permission of the publisher. For more information contact: www.WealthBuilderChallenge.com.

The author has made every effort to ensure the accuracy of the information within this book was correct at time of publication. The author does not assume and hereby disclaims any liability to any party for any loss, damage, or disruption caused by errors or omissions, whether such errors or omissions result from accident, negligence, or any other cause. The information contained within this book is strictly for educational purposes. If you wish to apply ideas contained in this book, you are taking full responsibility for your actions. The information is strictly given as the author's statements and is not meant to be taken as financial advice. Please consult a financial professional before making a change.

Printed in the United States of America

ISBN Hardcover: 978-0-9989966-5-3
ISBN eBook: 978-0-9989966-6-0

Library of Congress Control Number: 2017943942

Cover Design: popdesign✪
Interior Design: Ghislain Viau

To our beautiful wives, Marsha and Jocelyn, and to our amazing children! You are the reason we do what we do.

CONTENTS

CHAPTER 1: The Wealth Builder Challenge 1

CHAPTER 2: Don't Make More Than You Spend—Mastering the First Financial Basic 9

CHAPTER 3: From Budgets to Savings—Mastering Two Additional Financial Basics 21

CHAPTER 4: The Building Blocks of Investing 39

CHAPTER 5: Owning Stocks 49

CHAPTER 6: Owning Bonds 61

CHAPTER 7: Insurance—Protecting Yourself and Your Financial Plan 71

CHAPTER 8: Employee Benefits and Their Effect on Taxes 91

CHAPTER 9: Making Taxes Work for You 107

CHAPTER 10: How Fear Can Derail You from Your Pursuit of Wealth 121

CHAPTER 11: "I Wish I Had Met You Twenty Years Ago" 135

CHAPTER 1
THE WEALTH BUILDER CHALLENGE

Building wealth is a major challenge, and one of the best ways to manage that challenge is to develop a good plan from the beginning to avoid costly mistakes later. The Wealth Builder Challenge will focus on the most impactful areas of wealth building and provide you with new understanding and actionable steps to put you on a proven path to financial success.

As Grunden Financial Advisory, Inc., we have served hundreds of clients who have achieved financial success the old-fashioned way—through hard work and discipline. These individuals have achieved, or are on track to achieve, the goals most important to them. In this book, we have distilled our combined fifty-five years of wealth management experience into six core wealth-building principles:

1. Defer gratification: live beneath your means.
2. Recognize that the only free lunch is investment diversification.
3. For pennies on the dollar, protect yourself and your financial plan.
4. Do not leave money on the table; maximize your employee benefits.
5. Make tax law work for you.
6. Combined with the strategies outlined in this book, *time* and a reliable *process* are the most important ingredients of financial success.

As with anything in life, investment and sacrifice made early create dividends that last for years beyond the original commitment. Whether it is an exercise plan, a diet plan, or an investment plan, true and lasting success requires a lifestyle change, an attitude that you can and will make the choices necessary to change the course of your life. True change has to come from habits formed from within that put you in a position to succeed.

The Wealth Builder Challenge is a way of life. It is a framework for making wise choices and a method to channel available resources effectively. Ultimately it becomes who you are and enables you to live the life you envision for yourself.

Henrys and Stans

We've shared these simple principles with our clients for the past forty-two years, and we've seen these clients succeed. These types of people or couples are "HENRYs"—High Earners, Not Rich Yet[1]. On the other hand, we have seen others over the years who did not follow their plans or defer gratification, and who let price get in the way of long-term value. At Grunden Financial Advisory, Inc. we call these people or couples, "STANs"—Spend Today, All Now.

Stans seem to think no matter how much they spend beyond their resources, somehow things are going to magically work out. They are not necessarily Pollyannas, but they tend to exhibit characteristics that make them incapable of living within their means even in the face of imminent financial calamity.

You probably know or have met people like Stan and Henry over the years. Stan leases top-of-the-line luxury cars and lives in an impressive home. Henry, on the other hand, tends to drive a nice car, but not always a brand-new one; he has a nice house, but nothing extravagant. Stan buys the newest technology so he can show off his expensive gadgets; Henry buys high-quality products that serve his needs for many years. Stan takes numerous and pricey vacations; Henry goes on vacation a couple of times a year.

---

1 http://archive.fortune.com/magazines/fortune/fortune_archive/2003/06/23/344573/index.htm

To all outward appearances, Stan is very successful and Henry is solidly middle income, but is this true? Unfortunately, Stan is swimming in consumer debt to fulfill his temporary desires, but Henry is slowly and systematically building wealth to provide a financially secure future for himself and his family. Stan tends to spend all his money, whereas Henry is a high earner, but is not rich yet. As we learn more about Stan and Henry, it will become apparent which of them is better suited for long-term life success and wealth.

Susan and John

Susan is a client who was once a Stan and later became a Henry. Susan and her first husband made a lot of money. They had all the trappings of wealth: nice cars, a boat, a house in an exclusive neighborhood . . . and a whole lot of debt. Sadly, but inevitably, the pressures of debt and maintaining their lifestyle led to their divorce. In order to save her credit rating, Susan committed to being responsible for all of the debt left over from her marriage, even though she knew it would be difficult.

However, she quickly learned that she did not make enough money to support the debt *and* cover her living expenses, so she took a second job as a receptionist at a health clinic. Despite the life lesson she was learning by working two jobs to pay off her debt, Susan still did not always spend within her means.

But then one day she had an epiphany: She came to realize that she did not have to spend all of her money to enjoy life; shopping and spending did not bring the satisfaction she craved.

Susan was a creature of habit, with good self-control. She decided to open a savings account at her credit union, and began to derive gratification from spending less and saving more. After she built her savings account, some of her co-workers talked about their new experience with a financial planner . . . and that is how she met Ricky Grunden, Sr., CFP®. After getting to know each other and agreeing there was common ground and chemistry to work together, Susan and Ricky's first move was to tweak her 401(k) and open up a small investment account. It turned out she was perfectly suited to the financial planning process; she just needed a track to run on to clarify her thinking and implement her ideas.

Susan's professional financial planning relationship with Ricky Grunden, Sr. began about twenty-four years ago. The hard discipline of continually deferring gratification was Susan's; the planning and accountability was Ricky's. When she earned raises in her salary, she decided not to spend the extra cash. Instead, she increased her investing, even if only by a small amount.

Working with Ricky, Susan allocated her 401(k) contributions to a variety of investment choices for broad diversification. Susan faithfully stayed the course, taking advantage of company stock plans, investing, and setting aside a little extra whenever she could. At first her gains were small, but over time they grew.

Today, Susan is happily married to John. They are both in their early sixties and live securely in a home that is right for them. John is retired, while Susan's job skills remain in high demand. John maintains a nice home for Susan, and the two are fully enjoying the start of their retirement years. Their life today is a product of their decades of hard work, and a testament that devising a sensible financial plan really pays off.

Susan and John kept their eyes on their long-term goals and did not let the ups and downs of life steer them into reactive, short-sighted decisions. Instead, they remained steadfast in their commitment to their plan and stayed focused on the things they had control over. Now, over thirty years after the beginning of Susan's financial journey, she and John are millionaires. But are they financially secure?

Their goal in retirement income is $150,000 per year. Between their Social Security benefits and company pension plans, John and Susan know that they will receive approximately $96,000 a year in base retirement income. And all that planning, deferred gratification, and investing along the way has enabled them to accumulate a diversified investment portfolio of $1.7 million. If this story resonates with you, then you have the makings of a Henry—because a Stan would likely scoff and say that Susan just got lucky.

The Wealth Builder Challenge

If you are up for the Wealth Builder Challenge, this book is intended to help you succeed. In the chapters that follow, we lay out our step-by-step process, which we developed by helping people like Susan, John, and *you*. The Wealth Builder Challenge incorporates proven strategies to help you understand your relationship to money and set out a plan to accomplish your goals. Since everyone's financial situation and goals are different, what may be a good fit for you may not be a good fit for the next person. But one thing is certain: when you live by and understand our six principles, even if you fall short of your accumulation goal, you will be better off than you would have been with the hit-or-miss "your brother-in-law sold you what?" method most people end up employing in life.

This book focuses on five core strategies to live out the Wealth Builder Challenge principles:

- **Financial Basics—Understanding How the Pieces Work**
- **Investing**
- **Insurance**
- **Employee Benefits**
- **Taxes**

Focus on these five main strategies, and you will begin to see specific, actionable items that you can start working on today.

Later in the book, we also examine the emotional side of the Wealth Builder Challenge principles—how process beats intuition and fear. These chapters offer guidance on conducting the right kind of self-examination in order to better understand your personal relationship with money.

In 2008, Russ Alan Prince and Lewis Schiff wrote *The Middle Class Millionaire*,[2] a book that examines a rising and influential economic class in the United States. Defined by the authors as individuals with a net worth of $1 million to $10 million, the "middle-class millionaire" is America's new affluent class. They are defined not just by the assets they hold, but also by their values, and by the fact that they have earned their wealth rather than inheriting it.

The Wealth Builder Challenge is about what it takes to make you a middle-class millionaire. If that sounds good to you, read on.

---

[2] Russ Alan Prince and Lewis Schiff, *The Middle-Class Millionaire* (New York: Doubleday, 2008).

CHAPTER 2

DON'T SPEND MORE THAN YOU MAKE—MASTERING THE FIRST FINANCIAL BASIC

Every journey starts somewhere, and the Wealth Builder Challenge starts with getting your financial "house" in order. Although the financial basics are not flashy or glamorous, they are vital skills to learn and habits to create. In 1940, Albert E. N. Gray gave an inspirational speech that still holds true today. He was speaking to the National Association of Life Underwriters in Philadelphia—a speech that was written for life insurance professionals, but is transferrable to all walks of life. In this speech, titled "The Common Denominator of Success," Gray said, "The common denominator of success—*the secret of success* of every man who has ever been successful—lies in the fact that he *formed the habit* of doing things that failures don't like to do."[1]

You will see throughout this book true stories of how ordinary people formed habits that allowed them to build wealth. In this chapter, we examine the first of three financial basics.

Financial Basic One: Live Beneath Your Means

The very first step in the Wealth Builder Challenge is to live beneath your means, which entails that you spend less money than you earn. Americans tend to purchase so many things to create the illusion of a middle-class lifestyle that it becomes difficult to differentiate needs from wants. Building wealth requires not only making the distinction between needs and wants, but committing to a lifestyle below your income. It is important not to wait for your income to rise before making the commitment to live below your means, because time is the one thing you cannot make more of. Every day gained is an opportunity to implement wise financial strategies, even with the smallest contributions.

To begin living below your means, try eliminating some of your non-essential monthly expenses to see how that might affect your lifestyle. Maybe you have a few regular

---

[1] www.amnesta.net/MBA/thecommondenominatorofsuccess-albertengray.pdf_

monthly expenditures, such as yard fertilization ($45), Starbucks coffee ($25), and the premium cable package ($45 extra). None of those alone are large amounts, but combined they come to $115 per month. Even that may not seem like much, but since we have limited time to do what we want to do—build wealth—the true cost is not just $115: Over forty years, with an 8 percent return,[2] an investment of $115 per month will grow to $401,465. In this hypothetical example, the true cost of the yard, cable TV, and Starbucks is therefore $401,465, which means you have to either find another way to earn this money or simply do without other things in the future.

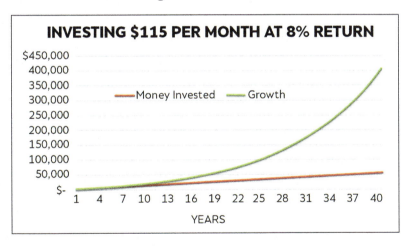

To be clear, there is nothing inherently wrong with treating yourself to a few luxuries from time to time. The problem

---

2 The absolute worst forty-year return for the S&P 500 stock index was 7.91 percent annualized, which began in September 1929 and ran through August 1969. See chapters 4–6 for more on investing.

arises when these things compromise your financial security and hinder your ability to build lasting wealth.

Consumer Debt

Consumer debt is often a symptom of the financial disease of living an unaffordable lifestyle. It can take a number of different forms:

I. Credit Cards

Credit cards are particularly dangerous, especially for people who have not yet mastered the habit of living beneath their means. The ability to swipe a credit card to fulfill any fleeting desire can make it more challenging to keep spending in check. If you have credit card debt and cannot describe what emergency necessitated the debt, then you need to pay close attention to creating the habit of living beneath your means (and also on budgeting, which we will discuss later). Besides encouraging you to spend too much, credit cards often charge very high interest rates; it is not uncommon to see interest rates on credit cards of 20 percent or higher. Until you have mastered living beneath your means, put a single credit card in a safe place, such as in a cup of frozen water in your freezer, in case of emergency, and shred any remaining cards.

Once you have developed the skills and instincts to live beneath your means, a credit card can be a convenient tool—and can even be used to build wealth. There are credit cards available that allow cardholders to earn 1 percent or more cash back simply by using the card to make purchases. If you can afford a purchase and plan on buying the item anyway, by all means use the credit card. The skilled Wealth Builder will not consider the cash back earned on the card as a bonus to spend, but will instead systematically put it toward his *directed savings*, another financial basic described later in the next chapter.

II. Auto Loans

Auto loans are often necessary for those beginning the journey laid out in the Wealth Builder Challenge, but beware of overspending on a vehicle. In order to sell more cars and make more on financing, dealers continue to increase the length of auto loans. Whereas a four- or five-year loan used to be standard, today you will often see six- or even seven-year notes advertised. Auto dealers will frame the longer financing solutions as a way to lower your monthly payments, but in reality these loans are designed to sell you a more expensive vehicle. If you cannot afford the payments on a four-year auto loan, then you may be looking at a car beyond your means.

A great way to maximize value in an automobile purchase is to buy a used car. Brand new automobiles depreciate immediately after they are purchased, losing thousands of dollars in value in the first year. As a Wealth Builder, there is no reason to pay this cost when you can easily assign it to someone else—that is, by letting the original owner of the automobile take the depreciation hit.

Another piece of advice for avoiding the auto loan trap: make sure you are buying a vehicle that will fit your family's needs for the next several years so that you can avoid having to change cars frequently. The vast majority of automobiles are depreciating assets—that is, they are worth less when you sell them than when you buy them. As such, making car purchases as infrequently as possible enables you to avoid wasting resources.

III. Mortgages

The largest purchase the vast majority of people will ever make is their primary residence. In fact, first-time homebuyers represented 32 percent of all residential sales[3] in 2016. And for most, that means a mortgage is necessary debt. Owning a home allows you to fulfill a basic human need—shelter. Remember that first and foremost, this is the main purpose for purchasing your primary residence.

Sometimes you will hear people saying that they made money on a house they only lived in for a couple of years because it increased in value. However, what many people fail to realize that the next house they will purchase probably increased in value just as much as their old house did

---

3 http://economistsoutlook.blogs.realtor.org/2017/01/30/first-time-homebuyers-slightly-up-at-32-percent-of-residential-sales-in-2016/

during that same period. In the end, the transaction likely netted them less money than simply buying the second house to begin with.

The reason they are unlikely to be better off is due to transaction costs associated with buying and selling real estate. Think about how many people are involved anytime you buy or sell a home: real estate agents, mortgage brokers, mortgage issuers, title companies lawyers, appraisers, and more. Procuring the services of those entities increases the cost of purchasing that home. It is quite possible to have a house you purchase go up in value, but your true goal should be to find a reasonably priced house in a good location that you will enjoy living in. The appreciation of your house is a secondary benefit after you have fulfilled the need for shelter.

It is hard to make a blanket statement on mortgages because so much depends on the interest rate and individual circumstances. However, there are two things to consider about mortgages:

Down Payment: If you can, put 20 percent down on the purchase of your home. This gives you immediate equity and obviates the requirement that you purchase private mortgage insurance (PMI). If you cannot put 20 percent down, consider "buying out" PMI. Instead of paying a monthly PMI fee until the equity in your home equals 20 percent, ask your mortgage broker how much it takes to pay off PMI as a lump sum today at a discount. As long as you commit to remaining in the house and do not refinance for a number of years, odds are you will come out ahead.

Prepayment of Mortgage: The value of prepaying a mortgage is simply a function of the mortgage interest rate net of any interest tax deduction. Generally, if over the long term you expect a larger rate of return from your investment portfolio than you are paying in interest on your mortgage, your money may be more effectively applied to investing than making extra payments on the mortgage. This means that rather than making extra payments on a mortgage with a 4 percent interest rate, you can be better off investing in a portfolio with a non-guaranteed expected 6.5 percent rate of return over time. Therefore, closely evaluate taking a thirty-year fixed-rate mortgage and contribute available pre-payment dollars to your investment program.

People often argue that prepaying a mortgage is really all about the numbers. Admittedly, it can be confusing to consider home appreciation, shortened mortgage payment schedules, and investments all in one decision. To simplify this, below are two graphs to help you visualize why prepaying a mortgage when mortgage rates are low may reduce household wealth in the end. Both graphs show a thirty-year mortgage at a 4 percent interest rate on a

$250,000 house. The scenario assumes the house increases in value or appreciates by the long-term inflation rate of 3 percent every year.

In the first scenario, we show the result of prepaying the mortgage by putting an extra $300 on every mortgage payment. With the extra $300 per month, the thirty-year mortgage is paid off in just over twenty-one years. At that point we assume the entire mortgage payment plus the $300 extra is invested at a non-guaranteed 6.5 percent expected rate of return for the remaining nine years of the original note. The end result is total wealth accumulation of $852,091 ($250,000 mortgage repaid + $364,211 home appreciation + $237,880 investment account = $852,091).

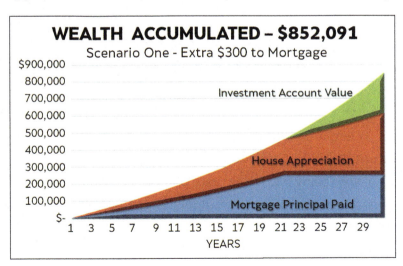

The only difference in the second scenario is that instead of paying an extra $300 to the mortgage, it is invested from the beginning at the same non-guaranteed 6.5 percent expected rate of return. This time the end result is accumulated wealth to the tune of $947,863. That is an extra $95,772! ($250,000 mortgage repaid + $364,212 home appreciation + $333,651 = $947,863) Not to mention the tax deduction for mortgage interest over the life of the loan and the effect of inflation on a fixed payment over 30 years.

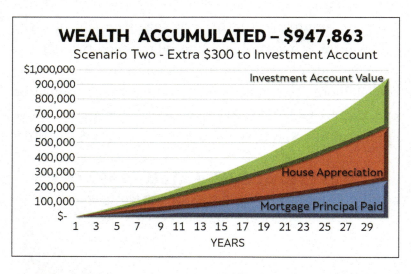

When it comes to a mortgage, learn to live within your means by limiting your total house payment to 28 percent of your *take-home* pay, after taxes and other paycheck deductions. The Wealth Builder understands that less home and more accumulation in tax-favored retirement accounts creates wealth while time is on their side.

When our friend Stan purchased a house, he made sure he was right up to his available mortgage limit. He wanted the largest house he could buy. Stan, like everyone else, can qualify for a much more expensive house than he can really afford. The mortgage company does not want you to keep your money; they want you to give it to them! Henry, following his plan to be more conservative in his home purchase, bought a smaller house than he qualified for and saved the extra money for his future every single month.

Small Steps, Big Payoff

Although living beneath your means can be challenging and even painful at times, it is an essential financial basic to master. Whether this means curbing your credit card spending or opting not to splurge on that brand-new BMW or extra square footage on a home, the small steps you take *today* to live beneath your means can lead to massive payoffs when it comes to building wealth for *tomorrow*. Read on!

Wealth Builder Challenge Takeaways

- Living beneath your means makes it possible to save money.

- Credit cards are a challenge for people who have difficulty with impulse control.

- Longer-term auto loans are expensive in the long run: if you cannot afford the payments on a four-year loan, you should buy a less expensive car.

- Buy a used car: Let someone else—the previous owner—incur the loss from the initial depreciation.
- Houses are for living in, not for trying to make a profit.

CHAPTER 3

FROM BUDGETS TO SAVINGS—MASTERING TWO ADDITIONAL FINANCIAL BASICS

In the previous chapter, we examined the first financial basic, living beneath your means. Now let us look at two other fundamentals to wealth building: budgeting and saving.

Financial Basic Two: Creating a Budget to Manage Cash Flow

Budget is a word that strikes terror into many people's hearts! One reason most people do not like to create a budget (or adhere to it after they create it) is that the process requires discipline. Successful Wealth Builders start with a fundamental budget, which entails an understanding of income and "required spending."

The first step in creating a budget is to determine your cash flow: where am I getting money from, and where is it going? The income you are going to budget is your take-home pay, after taxes and deductions. When you nail down your income, you move to the more difficult task of determining where the money is going—but do not worry, there are available tools to help you. If you use debit and/or credit cards, you can typically pull a comprehensive end-of-year report that breaks your spending down by category.

In the grand scheme of budgeting, what you really want to determine is how much money you have coming in, and from there, how much goes to *fixed expenses* (e.g., mortgage), how much goes to *flexible expenses* (e.g., groceries), and how much goes to *discretionary expenses* (e.g., entertainment, gifts, and eating out).

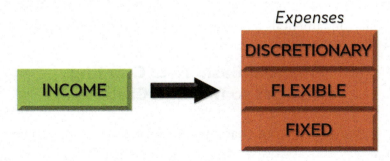

Generally speaking, you will have little *short-term* control over fixed expenses such as housing, transportation, debt payments, utilities, and insurance premiums. These expenses are easy to identify and budget for, but they should not be easily dismissed as set in stone! For example, if you have utility companies competing for your business, you can often find a better deal with a different company. Call your current provider and negotiate a better rate. Check your utility costs at least every couple of years. This goes for auto and homeowner's insurance, too: find an independent agent who will check your policies occasionally to see if there is a better deal out there. Shop around for lower rates, take control, and take pride in the small efforts that can help you save money so you can invest in your future.

Flexible expenses are not really optional, but they can be reined in as needed. For example, you have to buy groceries, but how much you spend is *flexible* to a point. Cutting out snack purchases and opting for store brands over brand-name foods can reduce a grocery bill.

Pure *discretionary expenses* need to be budgeted closely, since trouble often lurks in this spending category. A larger television is a "want," not a "need." What is required to build financial security is to create the habit of capturing a portion of your paycheck as early in life as you can, while consistently and systematically investing. "Wants" do not do this. This is not to say that you cannot get a larger television, but it should be planned and budgeted for.

Now that you know your income and your expenses, the difference between those two numbers is what you have available to save—or how far above your means you are living. If you have more expenses than income, take drastic measures now! Cut your discretionary expenses, reduce your flexible expenses, and shop around on your fixed expenses.

If you are struggling, seek professional guidance if necessary. When you are sick, you go to a doctor. So if your finances are ailing, why not consider a financial planner? It is important to bring your expenses down below your income to ever make progress toward your long-term goals. If your expenses are lower than your income, congratulations! You have already met one part of your goal by living beneath your means. Before discussing "Financial Basic Three," you need to learn about two additional budgeting concepts: *paying yourself first* and *lifestyle creep*.

Pay Yourself First

Once you have a surplus of income that exceeds the cost of expenses, then "pay yourself first." Automate the *directed savings* process by setting up a regular, repeating withdrawal from your checking account deposited to your savings, or directed toward your investments or debt (depending on your needs and circumstances). By doing so, you can now add investment deposits to your budget as a **fixed expense**. This is the first key to taking the Wealth Builder Challenge: you must consistently put away the money necessary to build wealth. Make it a habit, because you can never regain lost time. After enough time passes, saving will not even feel like an option anymore; it will become routine, and even fun. When you reach this point, you are well on your way to building wealth!

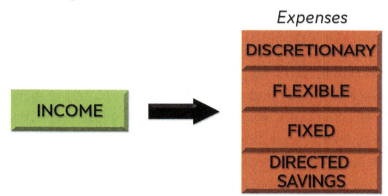

Once you begin to get serious about the process, you will probably wonder, "How much do I need to save?" The old standard was 10 percent of your income, but nowadays that is too low. More recently 15 percent has come to be regarded as the percentage of income to save, but is that enough? The answer really depends on your age and personal goals, but a qualified advisor can help you determine how much to save. Regardless, it is important that you start *now*. Every day of investing missed is a day that can never be recovered.

Lifestyle Creep

As people make more money, they spend more; it is just human nature. As they spend more money, they become adjusted to that new lifestyle, *making it hard to go back to spending less*. The problem is that the more expensive the lifestyle a person leads, the more they have to save to support it after retirement! As you make more, you should enjoy the fruits of your labor, but beware of letting your lifestyle creep up faster than your savings rate.

To avoid lifestyle creep, the next time you get a raise, save half of it. If your paycheck increases by $200 a month, invest $100 and put the other $100 in your budget to spend. *Voila!* You enjoy your newfound raise while combating lifestyle creep and accelerating your savings! It is not hard to do, but it requires conscious thought, discipline, and action. *Those who build wealth have discipline.* Be Henry, not Stan!

As soon as Henry got to the point in his career at which he started receiving bonuses and stock options, he began to divide his bonus and stock options four ways. First, he budgeted the appropriate amount to taxes (a fixed cost). Second, he gave 15 percent of the gross to his favorite charity. Third, he saved 35 percent for his retirement. Lastly, he splurged, spending 20 percent on discretionary items. He enjoyed the fruits of his labor, but also prepared for the future.

On the other hand, when Stan got his bonus, he spent the entire amount on discretionary purchases, squandering valuable time and an investment opportunity. Stan missed out on the opportunity to invest a portion of his bonus and have it grow and compound over decades.

Many middle-aged and retired clients regret not making these lifestyle changes sooner. Do not let time slip away from you. Take the Wealth Builder Challenge today, and put yourself on a better track to a more successful tomorrow.

Financial Basic Three: Directed Savings

Now that you have created your budget and are ready to automate your savings by paying yourself first, where do you invest? There is an order in which you should direct your money to get the most benefit from your savings. That specific order is referred to as *directed savings*.

401(k) Match

First, if you are eligible for a matching contribution to your 401(k), make sure you contribute enough to get the full match from your employer. This is free money for you, so do not leave it on the table! If after you make the contribution to your 401(k) you do not have any additional money for your *directed savings*, then you need to revisit your budget and trim your expenses.

A recent *Wall Street Journal* article[1] characterized the 401(k) as a retirement accumulation tool fallen short. The article cites "longer life spans, high fees and stock

---

1 Timothy W Manta, "The Champions of the 401(k) Lament the Revolution They Started," *Wall Street Journal*, January 2, 2017.

market declines" as the reasons the 401(k) is not turning out to be suitable for a large part of the working population. However, we have seen time and time again that the behavior of people (i.e., Stans) is more to blame. Stans choose to underfund their 401(k)s, and by doing so they fail to take advantage of a tax-deductible, tax-deferred opportunity whose value exceeds the cost of administration. Most important of all, Stans fail to stick with their investment plans regardless of whether the market is up or down. Henrys see the 401(k) as a wonderful opportunity to take charge of their futures and invest well for themselves. Henrys actually appreciate the down times in the market since they know they are accumulating more shares at lower prices.

People are driven by emotions, and without a strategy, emotion will almost always win—usually to the detriment of a solid investment program. Henry understands that 401(k)s work; you just have to *put the principles of investing to work within your 401(k)* to make them work for you. You have to find investable funds to move further in the Wealth Builder Challenge, and your 401(k) is the perfect place to start.

Emergency Fund

Second, build a fund that is immediately available in case of emergency. Most experts agree that three to six months of net spending is enough. (Net spending = Fixed Expenses + Flexible Expenses. By definition, discretionary spending is not a must.) If yours is a single-earner household, you put aside closer to six months of income in an emergency fund; a dual-earner household can make do with three months' income.

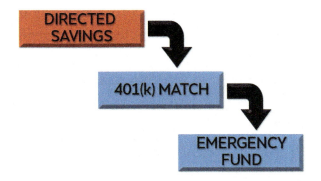

Debt

If you have credit card debt, or some other form of debt like excessive student loans or back taxes, you should now direct your automatic investing toward paying that debt down as soon as possible. Since debt payments are a fixed expense, you should at least make the minimum payments. Now that you are applying your directed savings to debt repayment, you will see the amount of debt reduce more quickly than when you were only making minimum payments.

It is exceptionally important to pay down your debt as quickly as possible. While the goal of the Wealth Builder Challenge is to reach financial security by leveraging your financial resources wisely, debt constantly works against you. Instead of having your money compound for your benefit, you are helping someone else's money compound by paying interest on your debt for the "privilege" of being a debtor.

Since debt payments are a fixed expense, paying off debt reduces the total amount of your fixed expenses. The money that you were dedicating to debt repayment can then be moved to the next directed savings goal, but be certain that you continue to live beneath your means and maintain your budget so you do not fall into the debt trap again. A mortgage and auto loan do not count as debt for these purposes, nor does a reasonable amount of student loan debt.

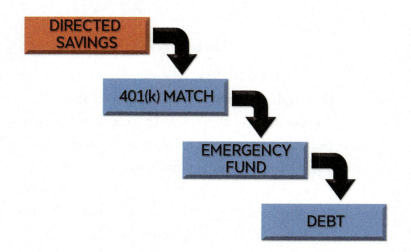

Retirement Savings

When it comes to funding retirement, you have three primary options for accomplishing your goal: retire later in life, spend less in retirement, or save more during your working years. The only one of these three options that will bring the added benefit of financial security is to save more. Saving more during your working career will also give you the option of retiring earlier, not later, and you will not have to spend less in retirement unless you want to.

You may have noticed our repeated references to losing time by waiting to invest. This is because of *the time value of money*. The time value of money is a fancy investing term for the concept of compounding interest. The more time there is for money to grow and compound, the larger it becomes.

The power of compounding interest is almost always underestimated. Look at how Henry used the time value of money to his advantage while Stan let time slip away. Henry put aside $5,500 each year for his Roth IRA from age twenty-two until age thirty-five—thirteen years. Stan waited to start saving until he was thirty-five, but he contributed the same $5,500 to his Roth IRA until he was sixty-five—thirty years. Both men are the same age and earned the same compounded 8 percent return[2] on their investments, but Henry only put

---

[2] The absolute worst forty-year return for the S&P 500 stock index was 7.91 percent annualized, which began in September 1929 and ran through August 1969. See chapters 4–6 for more on investing.

$71,500 in his Roth IRA while Stan put $165,000 in his Roth IRA. Since they both earned the same rate of return on their investments and Stan put in far more money, we would typically think he would have much more at age sixty-five. But thanks to the time value of money, Henry has twice the dollar amount in retirement as Stan: Henry actually has $1,284,821, while Stan has only $672,902!

The moral of the story? Don't be a Stan! Start investing whatever you can, as early as you can, as often as you can, and leave whatever you save alone for as long as you can! Do be a Henry!

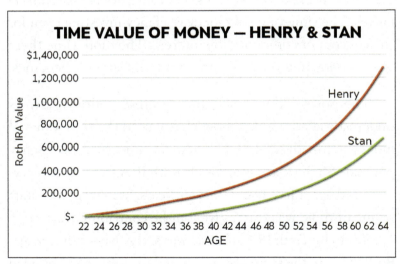

For many Americans who were retiring twenty years ago, retirement income was expected to consist of what was called the three-legged stool: 1/3 Social Security, 1/3 company pension income, and 1/3 personal savings. Those who are preparing for retirement today often have to come to terms with a vastly different retirement income mix.

First of all, pensions are quickly fading away. Today, only a few people have pensions that will provide a guaranteed income in retirement (with the exception of government employees). Simply put, going forward, the majority of Americans cannot count on a pension.

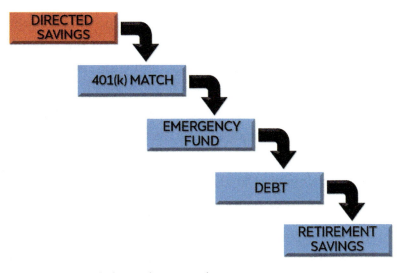

On top of that, the Social Security system is running a deficit, and changes are looming. Congress may take any number of steps to shore up the program for future generations. We do not expect Social Security to disappear, but future retirees would be wise to expect lower benefits than current retirees. Without pensions, and with the possibility of lower Social Security benefits for younger generations, we are looking at heavier reliance on personal savings. That means your retirement is primarily on you, and personal responsibility is paramount.

Where Do I Put Aside Retirement Savings?

There are many different types of accounts into which you can direct your savings. The most common ones are an individual or joint brokerage account, traditional 401(k) or IRA, and Roth 401(k) or IRA. Each type of account is ideal for certain individuals and circumstances, but without knowledge of your goals, your age, and your tax return, it is not possible to make a customized recommendation here and tailor choices specific for you. The following paragraphs are only meant to provide general overviews and guidelines for how to allocate retirement savings; we advise you to engage a professional to examine your unique situation in the context of your own personal financial plan.

For many people, contributing the maximum amount to a Roth IRA each year is the first step toward wealth building after getting any available 401(k) match. What makes a Roth IRA such a great retirement savings tool is its tax benefits—money put into a Roth IRA is never taxed again, nor is the growth of that money. In our example a couple of pages ago, Henry put $71,500 into his Roth IRA and ended up with $1,284,821. He could take the entire amount out of the account (assuming he was over 59½ years old) and not owe a penny in taxes.

A traditional 401(k) or IRA has a different tax benefit from a Roth 401(k) or IRA, and is more beneficial to people with higher incomes. Contributions to a traditional 401(k) or IRA typically allow for a tax deduction at the time the funds are deposited into the account, and when the money is withdrawn in retirement it is taxed as ordinary income. Getting a tax deduction means you do not have to pay income taxes on the amount you contribute, which is great in the short term, but the original contribution and any growth in the account is taxed when withdrawn. Keep in mind Roth IRA contribution income limits. If you make too much money, you can't contribute to a Roth IRA. For 2017, if you pay tax on more than $187,000 you won't be able to fully fund a Roth IRA.

After your Roth IRA is funded you should look at your employee benefits package to see if there is any other "free company money" available, and begin funding those plans if appropriate (see chapter 8 for more details on employee benefits). Once employee benefits are reviewed, go back to the 401(k) and begin funding above and beyond what is required to capture the employer match, up to the maximum contribution limit of $18,000 ($24,000 if over age fifty).

In addition to the traditional tax-deductible 401(k) contribution, some 401(k) plans offer a Roth 401(k) option, which functions like a Roth IRA for tax purposes. Before funding the traditional or Roth 401(k), evaluate your tax situation to determine whether the tax deduction of a traditional 401(k) contribution may be more beneficial than tax-free growth in a Roth 401(k). This can be difficult to determine, so it may be best to consult a tax advisor or personal financial planning advisor.

If Henry is doing well and still has money left over after funding his Roth IRA and 401(k), he will begin to fund an individual or joint brokerage account with after-tax funds. There is no special tax treatment for these accounts—you pay taxes on gains as you capture them. However, you also have the advantage of being able to access the money in the investment account at any point and manage your taxes along the way.

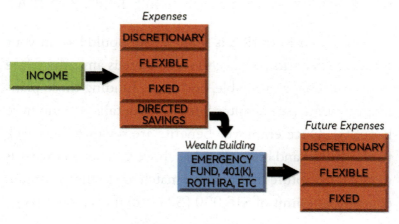

College Savings

You may have noticed that we have not discussed saving for college expenses; that omission is not a mistake. Some people will neglect their own retirement savings to give their children the best possible education. While they only want

From Budgets to Savings—Mastering Two Additional Financial Basics

to see their children succeed, this is shortsighted thinking. First and foremost, it is your responsibility to prepare for retirement; the US government will likely give your family a low-cost loan for college expenses, but no one will loan you money for retirement if you end up falling short.

Does it really benefit your children to pay for their college if you run out of money in retirement and end up forfeiting your financial dignity when they end up supporting you? Though having your kids take out student loans is not the ideal way to pay for college, it is far better than becoming dependent on your children in retirement.

Personal responsibility is a virtue, and that means it is also necessary for your children to take responsibility for their own futures; only by doing so will they become the next generation of Henrys.

If you are well on your way to a secure retirement, then it is time to discuss the best way to save for college for your children. Just as with saving for retirement, there is no single, correct way to save for future education expenses. Education savings is beyond the scope of this book, but a financial planning advisor can provide you with personalized advice.

So now that you are set up with a 401(k), a Roth IRA, and perhaps a joint brokerage account, turn to the next chapter, in which we will focus on how to invest these hard-earned funds.

Wealth Builder Challenge Takeaways

- Time is the most important element in the wealth accumulation phase.
- Lost time is not recoverable. One can always make more money, but not more time.
- Live below your means by not overextending yourself on a car, a house, or expensive vacations.
- Manage your cash flow by having a budget. Separate your budget into categories: fixed, flexible, and discretionary expenses.
- When pay raises come, save or invest half the raise to minimize lifestyle creep.
- Maintain three to six months of expenses in an emergency fund.
- Begin saving and investing for retirement now.
- Pay yourself first by:
  o Contributing to your 401(k) to receive the full employer match
  o Funding a Roth IRA
  o Maxing out 401(k) contributions
- Send extra money to an individual or joint account.

CHAPTER 4
THE BUILDING BLOCKS OF INVESTING

Now that we have covered the financial basics, you are ready to put the directed savings portion of your income and budget to work building wealth. First, remember that the Wealth Builder Challenge is about *building* wealth over time, and it is a challenge that occurs over the course of a career—years and decades, not weeks and months.

Financial Basics as the Foundation of a House

It's often said that wealth building is like building a house; this is a cliché, but only because the metaphor is an apt one. The financial basics are the foundation that supports the house. A well-built foundation will not easily crumble, and with some maintenance can last hundreds of years. With the foundation in place, actual construction can begin. Built right, this home will shelter your family for this lifetime, and perhaps even into the next generation.

Brick by Brick: Automatically Deducted Directed Savings

The best way to build wealth is to dedicate portions of your *directed savings* automatically to investments. This chapter will explain what this means and discuss the importance of paying yourself first by investing every month, and the importance of staying the course. We will also explain the different types of investments, and we will describe the

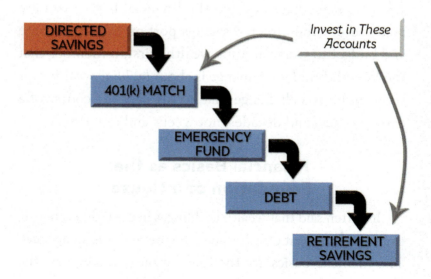

building blocks of an investment portfolio and where they fit into your Wealth Builder Challenge.

Lay One Brick at a Time: Pay Yourself First

In the Wealth Builder Challenge, paying yourself first is not optional. Consider the act of saving for a fixed expense; in other words, think of your $400-a-month contribution to your investment account as a bill that you must pay, a fixed expense. When you do this every month, your house begins to take shape.

The idea of investing a set amount of money on a regular and systematic basis is known as *dollar cost averaging*. Regardless of how your investments are performing—going up, going down, going nowhere—you keep making monthly contributions with the goal of accumulating shares. By doing so, the "costs" of the shares average out over time. Each time you put money into your dollar cost averaging program, you are laying a brick on the foundation of your financial house. Dollar cost averaging is not risk mitigation, or a guarantee that your account will appreciate over time, but it is an excellent way to accumulate shares and build wealth.

Stans often worry that they are entering the stock market at its high-water mark, and fearing short-term losses, they hesitate or fail to invest. This fear can be debilitating and counterproductive: the longer the money sits on the sidelines, the more convinced Stans become that they cannot invest because a downturn is inevitable.

We have seen this exact scenario play out many times with the Stans who come to us seeking advice. For example, after the stock crash of 2008, it took the market about four and a half years to return to its previous high set in October 2007. When the market hit bottom and started to shoot up, the Stans who listened to the financial talking heads did not believe the recovery would persist . . . but it did. They did what investors left to themselves always do—they sold at or near the bottom, reasoning that it was better to walk away with something rather than "lose it all."

Now the tough part (and it is always the tough part because we don't know the future): the Stans fear when the market is rising that it will turn and go down—or when it is falling that it will continue to go down. Sitting on piles of cash, they just cannot bring themselves to invest, and to this day many are still waiting for the "right time." This type of fear can prevent otherwise dedicated investors from entering the market.

The problem is that we have no idea what the market will do in the short term, but Henrys love a systematic investment program, and dollar cost averaging keeps their focus on the correct thing—plodding along, accumulating shares. Because the Wealth Builder Challenge is not won overnight, it is best to keep building your house, moving forward, and investing according to your plan in all kinds of markets, up and down.

By committing a relatively small amount on a regular basis, dollar cost averaging makes the decision to stay the course easier and can take the emotional aspect out of investing. Rather than futilely attempting to time investments when the market is down, a Henry instead automatically adds shares to his portfolio month in and month out, regardless of what the market does. As a result, market downturns actually become helpful, as each new "discounted" purchase buys more shares! Like many aspects of investing, buying when stocks are falling runs counter to our emotions, but dollar cost averaging in a down market allows you to buy more stocks when they are less expensive!

Staying the Course

In the first decade of the twenty-first century, the American economy experienced two severe recessions. Investors entering the market in 2000, when tech stocks were high, rode a decade-long rollercoaster to the very bottom in 2009—the most severe decline in stock prices since the Great Depression. During that ten-year period, one dollar invested in the S&P 500 (the 500 largest US companies) returned ninety-one cents—a loss of nine cents, even with dividends reinvested. Not promising.

Evaluated through the lens of dollar cost averaging, however, the picture looks a little different. An investor who participated in a dollar cost averaging program in the

S&P 500 over the same period and reinvested all dividends would have achieved a return of 1.36 percent annualized—their dollar would have grown to $1.14. The point is this: even really bad times for the market can earn money if you remain committed to systematic contributions.

What if we broadened the time horizon for a full fifteen years, from the beginning of 2000 through 2014, when the S&P 500 grew an annualized 4.24 percent with all dividends and capital gains reinvested, equating to a total return of 86 percent? On the other hand, to illustrate the power of time and commitment to dollar cost averaging over the entire fifteen-year period, one dollar would have grown to $3.32, for an 8.33 percent annualized and a total return of almost 100 percent![1]

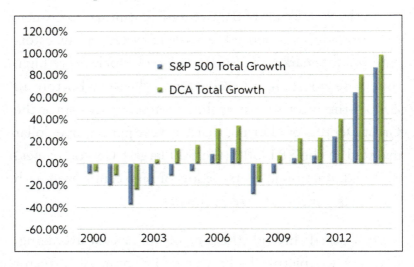

---

[1] S&P 500 returns from the DFA Returns Program 2.0

Dollar cost averaging can take the emotion out of investing, and though it is not guaranteed, may produce better returns over time.

Types of Investments: Stocks and Bonds—the Building Blocks of an Investment Portfolio

Stocks and bonds are the two primary asset classes used to construct investment portfolios. There are three primary reasons for building a portfolio using both stocks and bonds. First, depending on the amount of risk one can stomach, a portfolio must balance the ups and downs in the market commonly referred to as volatility. Stock prices tend to be volatile (move up and down dramatically) in the short term, while bonds are more stable. Second, the respective values of stocks and bonds often (but not always) move in opposing directions, and investing in both helps to smooth out the performance of a portfolio if stocks go down while bonds go up. Third, combining stocks and bonds allows an investment advisor to help tailor a financial plan to your personal appetite for investment risk.

Spread the Risk Between Stocks and Bonds When Necessary

Fundamentally, an investment portfolio must be diverse; that is, it must include different asset classes to participate in returns and spread risk. When we create portfolios tailored to our clients' goals and financial plans, they typically include US stocks and bonds and international stocks and bonds.

At the portfolio level, diversification refers to spreading stock risk between domestic and international stocks, and then further reducing risk, as appropriate, with bonds. A rule of thumb has circulated in financial publications for several years concerning how much of a portfolio should be allocated to stocks and how much to bonds: subtract your age from 120 to find the percentage of stocks you should have in your portfolio. This is overly simplistic; the best approach is a portfolio developed in consideration of your individual goals and according to your own personal financial plan.

If you want to build wealth and are very young in the accumulation phase of your life, your diversified portfolio should be 100 percent stocks, or very close to it. But even

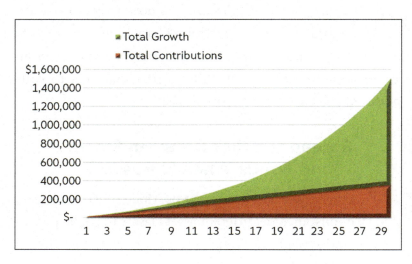

with a portfolio of 100 percent stocks, you should still diversify across US and international stocks.

Consider a thirty-year-old Wealth Builder investing $1,000 per month in a diversified stock market portfolio averaging an 8 percent annualized return. By the time our Wealth Builder Challenger reaches age sixty, she would have invested $360,000, and would have a portfolio worth $1,500,000!

Wealth Builder Challenge Takeaways

- Start as soon as you can. You cannot make up for lost time, and you cannot afford to lose any more time by delaying. Start today.
- Establish a dollar cost averaging strategy to regularly and systematically invest money in stocks regardless of recent performance. It is never too late to start this program!
- Invest in short-term, high-quality bonds to mitigate the risk associated with owning stock.
- Younger investors should weight their portfolios heavily toward stocks, gradually adding bonds when their personal goals and financial plans dictate.
- By combining the long-term growth of stocks with dollar cost averaging and reinvesting dividends, you are effectively laying the bricks of your financial house.

CHAPTER 5
OWNING STOCKS

Everybody has heard about the stock market, but what exactly is it? Generally speaking, the stock market is the public marketplace organized where the owners of shares of publically traded companies exchange them for an agreed-upon price. For example, if an investor owns 100 shares of stock in Johnson & Johnson, they actually own a piece of the company. As an owner, the stockholder is entitled to a portion of the income the company earns. If the company is successful over time, the stockholder's shares in the company can also grow in value. Stocks are sometimes referred to as equities.

Think about this: Businesses that bring value to everyday citizens can be yours to own. A free-market economy with a stock market open to citizens is the ultimate way to spread and build wealth; anyone can be a business owner! Capitalism is the greatest economic system the world has ever known to generate wealth, and the stock market is a highly efficient system to spread the wealth to those willing to participate. If your grandparent or great-grandparent chose to invest $1,000 across the total stock market on January 1, 1926, three years before the Great Depression began, and then never touched the investment, it would have been worth over $4.5 million dollars at the end of 2016.[1] The key to successful investing is to have a plan, broadly diversify over various asset classes, and not become emotionally attached to your money (which is difficult, since we are emotional beings).

Is It Gambling?

Some people say putting money in the stock market is like gambling, but it really isn't. Gambling is betting on a chance for an outcome, but buying stocks in a diversified portfolio makes you an owner, an overseer of your investments. As owner you can vote your shares, attend annual shareholder meetings, review annual reports governed by the SEC and accounting standards, and even get quarterly updated reports from outside analysts assigned to track your company.

---

1 As measured by the CRSP 1-10 index, a good proxy for how the overall stock market performed, from 12/31/1926 through 12/31/2016.

Owning Stocks

Gambling in the stock market, on the other hand, is when you "bet" on a hot stock or the direction of the market. That is not investing. That is speculating—which is gambling.

Early in Ricky's career, a friend amassed about $25,000 and entrusted him with the responsibility of managing it. Things were moving along okay, but not great—just okay. One day this friend called and asked Ricky to liquidate his account. Of course Ricky wanted to know why, so he asked, "Are you moving your money to another broker"?

"No," he replied, "a man I met in church is letting me in on a ground-floor opportunity. Time is short, and I have to get the funds there as quickly as possible or I lose the chance to be a player."

It's amazing how easily even rational people can get sucked into these schemes. Usually there is a relationship with a degree of trust, and a pitch that appeals to our natural greed—getting something bigger, better, and quicker for less. It can happen to anyone, but this type of get-rich-quick scheme seems to *really* attract Stans. It's all about the excitement.

But a Henry is wiser. Henrys have a plan and understand that excitement and complexity in an investment proposal usually indicates increased risk, and this type of risk is unnecessary to success. We call "opportunities" like this *uncompensated risk*, meaning you take a risk that is not easily measured—as compared to a portfolio in which risk can be measured based on past volatility and returns. In such a portfolio you have a good idea of what your downside and upside look like over time, and the odds are that your investment meets those expectations. All you have to do to succeed in investing is stay in the game to get your fair share and follow the rules:

- Risk and return are related
- There is no free lunch
- Complexity equals risk and increased costs
- Fear and greed drive poor investment decisions

Beware of any offer that sounds too good to be true. We have all seen these offers before, and they are alluring, but stay wise, stay away, and be a Henry by sticking to your plan and staying the course.

Getting back to Ricky's friend, it turns out his "contact" had invented a type of epoxy glue that could seal leaks on small fishing boats. The reason for the hurry, he claimed, was that the product was soon to be distributed by the largest discount store in the US, a name we all know. Sadly, it was a con, and this man lost his $25,000. Don't gamble, and don't be drawn in by get-rich-quick schemes. Don't play, because it is not necessary to succeed in life and investing.

Finally, pay close attention to investments promoted as a way to shelter against taxes or provide other tax benefits.

While some investments do provide legal tax benefits, these benefits are not without costs. Capitalism and the free market allow investment money to flow to its best expected return, and these investments are no different. If tax-sheltered investments were such a fabulous deal, the wealthy would quickly bid up their price and lower their value. Often investments promoted for their tax benefits are opaque, have substantial internal costs, lack liquidity, and do not outperform standard investments even after accounting for taxes over time.

What to Know About Stock Risk

Simply put, the risk of investing in stocks refers to how the prices of stocks go up and down, and in a worst-case scenario stocks may even become worthless due to bankruptcy, as happened with Enron in 2000 and General Motors in 2008. These two examples are extremes, but such events can and do occur. That is why Henrys choose broadly diversified portfolios and don't put all their eggs in one basket. Stans, on the other hand, are invariably drawn to the new startup or hot stock tip that sounds too good to be true . . . and in most cases it *is* too good to be true. But Stans think that somehow they have an inside track and are engaged with the smart money.

On the other hand, considering a long-term time horizon, the primary risk of investing in a broadly diversified portfolio of stocks is that you may be forced to withdraw funds when the stock market is down, causing a guaranteed loss—which is another reason your emergency fund is so important.

Let's consider another example of our two friends, Henry and Stan. Henry understands the ups and downs of the stock market, so for money he expects to need soon he puts aside $50,000 into a savings account. He ends up only needing $25,000, so he takes the remaining $25,000 and invests it in a broadly diversified portfolio. He hopes that within seven to ten years his $25,000 will have grown back to the original $50,000.

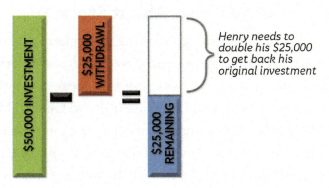

Henry needs to double his $25,000 to get back his original investment

Stan, on the other hand, does not take into consideration that short-term drops in the stock market are normal; he just wants to try to make money fast. He invests the same $50,000 in the stock market, knowing he will need to withdraw some of it in a few months. To Stan's surprise, when the time comes to withdraw that $25,000 he needs, the stock market has gone down in value. His original $50,000 investment is now worth $30,000, and he now needs to

Owning Stocks

spend most of the remaining balance. With only $5,000 remaining, it will to take Stan about thirty years to grow $5,000 back into his original $50,000.

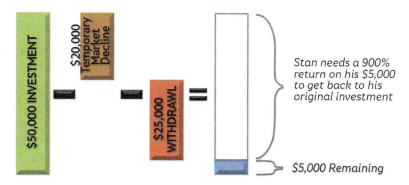

Stan's situation could have been avoided by understanding the short-term risks of the stock market's constant ups and downs. Of course, that is why a Wealth Builder Challenger like Henry has his financial house in order, with a fully funded emergency fund in place! He doesn't have to pull money from his stocks at an inopportune time.

Another risk associated with stocks is the single-stock risk, or the risk associated with owning a significant amount of any one stock. While the stock market as a whole benefits from huge investment returns over long periods of time, the fact is many companies come and go during those periods. Any company can go bankrupt; think General Motors, Fannie Mae, and Lehman Brothers, to name several in recent history. And of course, when companies fail, that almost always results in a total loss for shareholders.

Single-stock risk is easy to mitigate through diversification—and some consider buying small pieces of thousands of other companies to be the only true free lunch. Diversification is easily achieved by investing in mutual funds or exchange traded funds (ETFs). If you are not familiar with mutual funds and ETFs, think of them as a way for investors to pool their monies together for the benefit of buying in bulk. Clients often tell us, "I don't want to invest in mutual funds. You only get the market. I want individual stocks, and I want them diversified." Even if you had the money (which most people don't), buying one or two stocks in each industry is not a diversified portfolio; mutual funds and ETFs make diversifying much easier.

What to Look for When Investing in Stocks Through Mutual Funds

Diversification is a good practice when investing in stocks to build wealth, and understanding these three insights enables you to cut through the advertising hype and determine whether you are investing in a well-managed portfolio. All three of these secrets will put money in your pocket, and they do not depend on the uncertainty of the market for you to reap rewards:

- **Choose Low Turnover.** Turnover is how much a mutual fund manager buys and sells and trades the portfolio. You want to select the funds that minimize trading, because it seldom leads to improved performance, adds to cost, and generally increases capital gains distributions and associated taxes. Bad for you.

- **Choose a Low Expense Ratio.** A low expense ratio is the price you pay for the manager of your mutual funds or ETFs. A lower expense ratio tends to be an indication of proven systems and processes.

- **Choose the Number of Stocks Owned.** The fund should have several hundred different stocks, or better yet, several thousand. Stay away from funds that concentrate their holdings in a handful of stocks. These funds advertise manager stock-picking acumen or "best ideas," but in many cases they simply engender uncompensated risk, and over time their performance may not measure up to their benchmarks.

Just as it is important to find a fund that minimizes trading, it is even more important to determine your investment strategy in advance of investing, and stick to it. Resist the urge to trade your own portfolio. When you buy and sell there are costs, and outside of a retirement plan there are usually tax consequences. Your pathway to a successful investment experience is understanding your goals, choosing diversified investments, and focusing on the things you can control or change. Behavior is controllable; the direction of the world is not.

Understanding How Dividends Work

Dividends represent the cash distributions a company makes to its owners, the shareholders. We do not believe dividends are the holy grail of investing, but they are a definite benefit to being a shareholder. Just as you dollar cost average to invest in stocks regularly, dividends reinvested back into your stock funds help you build wealth. While you are buying stocks on a monthly basis through your dollar cost averaging program, your stocks help you buy even more shares on a regular basis through reinvested dividends! As time passes and your investment grows, so does the dividend and the number of shares the dividend buys.

Wealth Builder Challenge Takeaways

- The rule of law and private property rights form the foundation for capitalism, and you can participate in this growth of wealth by owning stocks.

- Staying the course, regardless of the market's ups and downs, is the wisest long-term strategy.

- Careful, prudent investment in the stock market is *not* gambling.

- Reckless, speculative betting on "tips" or currently hot stocks *is* gambling.

Owning Stocks

- Use mutual funds or ETFs to invest in stocks rather than buying stocks individually. Look for low turnover, low expenses, and the number of stocks owned.
- Beware of any offer that sounds too good to be true.

CHAPTER 6
OWNING BONDS

Bonds are not as exciting as investing in stocks, and you might be tempted to skim the next few pages... but don't. Bonds have a place in certain situations and with different types of investors. Be a Henry and add to your investor knowledge by reading on.

A bond is an obligation or debt a government or a company owes to the owner of the bond. While individuals get loans from banks when they need money, large organizations go straight to the public, bypassing the bank. Typically, bonds make an interest payment to the bondholder every six months. When the bond matures or is called away, bondholders receive the bond's face value back as repayment of the loan. Bonds are commonly referred to as fixed-income investments and are considered safer than owning stocks for two reasons: First, even if a company is struggling—that is, if it is experiencing declining or flat profits and falling share prices—the company will do everything in its power to make bond payments. It does this for three reasons: to protect its credit rating, to ensure that it is able to return to the market to borrow in the future, and because it is legally obligated.

Second, bondholders have higher standing in the capital structure of a company. Thus, if the company has to declare bankruptcy, bondholders will be paid from the resulting liquidation before shareholders, if a shareholder gets paid anything at all.

The downside is that bonds do not offer the same potential returns that stocks do. Risk and return are related, and as with everything else in the world, there is no free lunch. Bonds are less risky than stocks, and therefore do not generate the long-term returns associated with stocks. For example, consider Henry: Ten years ago, he purchased an iPod and was convinced Apple was really onto something. He decided to invest in Apple, but did not really appreciate the difference between stocks and bonds. Henry did what many people do when making a decision they are not sure of: he split the difference, investing $10,000 in Apple stock and $10,000 in Apple bonds. Henry bought the bonds at face value, and they were paying 5.5 percent interest. Assuming that the bonds matured in ten years, Henry would have earned 5.5 percent per year. By holding the bond to maturity, Henry simply could not make a higher return—the bond ceiling was capped at 5.5 percent. His ownership stake in Apple, on the other hand, turned out to be a good investment. Between 2005 and 2015, Apple stock produced an almost 39 percent annualized return! Henry's $10,000 had become $250,000.

The primary purpose of bonds in an investment portfolio is to reduce the overall risk to an appropriate level. Remember, we are using risk to describe the volatility (ups and downs) inherent in a portfolio. One of the principles of investing is that risk and return are related, so the more return you want to earn on your portfolio, the more risk (volatility) you will need to accept. History has shown a portfolio composed of 100 percent stocks provides a solid *long-term return*. To get that return, however, one has to stay committed to an investment plan, and not everyone wants or needs to accept the associated ups and downs.

As a Wealth Builder like Henry ages and approaches the achievement of his long-term goals, he may want to consider slowly reducing his stock exposure to a more balanced level—that is, reducing his investment in stocks and adding more bonds. Certainly a number of variables will affect this decision, such as personal and family health, standard of living, and perceived life expectancy, but the point is that bonds can play an important role in smoothing out the ups and downs in a portfolio, even for those with a high tolerance for risk.

For example, consider our client James, who began to behave like a Henry during his early thirties and remained 100 percent committed to stocks due to his long-term time horizon and his steady employment. James retired at the age of fifty-nine from his position as managing director of communication products for one of the largest semiconductor companies in the country. James lived through the ups and downs of the '90s market, the dot-com crash, and the Great Recession of 2008. But when he retired he no longer had a steady income to cover his living expenses.

We analyzed James' retirement plan and discovered that he had an 82 percent probability of success to age 100 (meaning that he could live to that age without running out of money), even if we reduced his stocks to 60 percent of his assets. In meeting with James, we illustrated this idea as "The Bucket Approach." Sixty percent of his allocation went into the stock bucket, and 40 percent into the bond bucket. This meant that no matter how the stock market might go up or down, there would be enough money in the bond bucket to secure his standard of living for over twelve years. Bear markets last on average fifteen months[1] (the longest bear market, during the Great Depression, lasted

---

1 http://www.cnbc.com/2015/08/24/8-things-you-need-to-know-about-bear-markets.html

thirty-four months[2]), giving James sufficient confidence to stay the course and sleep at night. This is a simple illustration to communicate the very important role of bonds in a portfolio.

Market Interest Rates, Bond Quality, Bond Duration, and Diversification

Bonds can actually be a very complicated investment to understand; their covenants and disclosures are written in legalese and run to hundreds of pages. For the purpose of this book, however, it is important for you to understand these four principles: Market Interest Rates, Bond Quality, Bond Duration, and Diversification.

Market Interest Rates

The value of a bond moves in the opposite direction of interest rates. When market interest rates go up, bond prices go down, making your bond portfolio worth less. When interest rates go down, bond prices go up, making your bond portfolio worth more. This is all the successful Wealth Builder absolutely must know about the interaction between bonds and interest rates . . . but it is also important to understand that at the time of this writing, interest rates are at the bottom of a thirty-five-year low, and interest rates are flat to increasing.

---

[2] As measured by the S&P 500 after reaching a high in August 1929 through the low of June 1932.

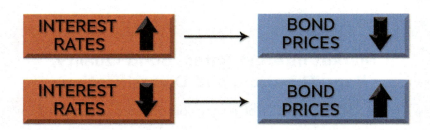

Bond Quality

The *quality* of a bond refers to the ability of its issuer to repay the bond as promised. Bond quality is graded on a spectrum depending on the likelihood that the issuer will make the bond payments. A high-quality bond is one issued by a company or government regarded as highly likely to repay. A low-quality or "high yield" bond is issued by a company or government that is more suspect, perhaps because it is facing some sort of headwind or is perceived as having the potential to default on its bonds (i.e., stop paying).

The lower quality a bond is, the higher the interest payment will be in relation to high-quality bonds—this again is the risk-and-reward relationship. Additionally, low-quality bonds have a much higher probability of permanently losing value due to bankruptcy or default than high-quality bonds, making them riskier and more volatile.

Low-quality bonds also have a tendency to move up and down with the *stock* market, making them riskier investments to include with a stock-heavy portfolio. Low-quality bonds tend to ride the market because their issuer, a "suspect" entity, is considered less likely to default when the economy and stock market are going strong. On the other hand, a tough economy makes it far more likely that a struggling company will default on its bonds. When investing in high-yield bonds, investors often hold an instrument that changes value similarly to stocks, but without the potential to generate as much return. Unlike high-quality bonds, low-quality bonds do little to reduce volatility in a portfolio.

Bond Duration

Long-term bonds are defined as those with a repayment period longer than ten years. We believe that unless interest rates are extremely high, as they were in the '80s, investing for higher returns is best done through stocks, which have historically outperformed long-term and low-quality bonds. Investors who wish to lower risk in their portfolios should acquire high-quality bonds with short or intermediate maturity to balance their portfolios. Let stocks be the main driver of returns, and let bonds mitigate overall risk.

Bond Diversification

Some investors really like the idea of having a portfolio of individual bonds, but just as it is difficult to truly diversify a stock portfolio, the same is even more true with individual bonds. At least with stocks, markets are considered to be efficient, meaning the price quote you see is very close to what a willing seller and a willing buyer would pay for the stock. But the bond market is different; it is not efficient unless the bond is a new issue. Bonds sold on the secondary market are priced a lot like homes: If you're selling your home, you do a neighborhood market survey, set the price as high as possible, and put out a "For Sale" sign. The buyer comes around, does their evaluation, and offers their lowest possible price, and the dance goes on until one party walks away or both parties agree on a price, usually somewhere in the middle.

Buying individual bonds is difficult because the buyer has almost no way of knowing what the bond they are buying is worth, or whether they are paying a good price. And once again, think of your competitors. There are bond funds that run billions of dollars in their portfolios, and one has to wonder why a bond is even available to small investors in the secondary market at all. How does the individual buyer of bonds (or a broker, for that matter) even hope to get a fair price for a bond when they have to compete with the internal research teams and quantity discount purchases of these mammoth mutual funds and ETFs? It is just not possible. Paying twenty basis points or less to a well-run bond fund is worth the price to know you are at least joining an elite competitor and not competing in a loser's game.

Wealth Builder Challenge Takeaways

- Bonds offer lower returns than stocks—but also lower risks.
- The presence of bonds in a portfolio reduces overall risk.
- Invest in short-term, high-quality bonds to mitigate the risk associated with owning stock.
- The value of bonds moves in the opposite direction of interest rates.
- The true value of a bond can sometimes be difficult for the buyer to determine.
- Low-quality bonds provide higher returns, but the risk is commensurately higher.

CHAPTER 7
INSURANCE—PROTECTING YOURSELF AND YOUR FINANCIAL PLAN

A properly designed insurance program can make your financial plans self-completing in the event of a sudden and unexpected loss. In the following paragraphs, Ricky Grunden, Sr. illustrates this for us by explaining, from his heart, the reason he carries a large life insurance policy—his wife, Marsha.

> My wife is a beautiful woman, and she has given our family eight beautiful children, who are now adults productively living their lives. Early in our marriage, when we were young, it was hard for me to afford the

cost of life insurance, but I always thought it was worth it. I never thought of our life insurance as a morbid idea or a nuisance; rather, it represented a love letter from me to Marsha. If something were to happen to me, I wanted her to know that the sacrifices we'd made over the years to save a little here and a little there would not be lost just because I didn't make it home from work one day. I wanted her to know that even though I might never again hold her at night, I would still hold her and the family together every day because I had done the responsible thing and secured her future through insurance. I'm sure most people do not view their insurance policies as "love letters," but I do.

Now, forty years after our vows, I am still making it home from the office each day. But without our complete insurance package, in the last three years alone we would have experienced major financial setbacks in the form of hail damage to our home, a couple of fender benders, family medical challenges, and other important insurance events. I suspect that all in, the above insurance protection represents close to $1.8 million dollars! So often the miraculous ability to transfer risk to a third party for pennies on the dollar simply by entering into a contract is misunderstood, or viewed as a necessary evil. The Henrys will understand the beauty of insurance; I expect the Stans will think I am crazy.

Insurance—Protecting Yourself and Your Financial Plan

As we said earlier, even the best financial plans cannot control or predict how outside forces will affect our lives, for good or for ill, but the wise application of insurance, the third strategy, helps to mitigate the risk of overwhelming loss that life presents from time to time.

Most insurance policies fall into two broad categories: 1) property and casualty (P&C), and 2) life and health (L&H). The most common P&C insurance policies are automotive and homeowner's, and there are also umbrella and commercial insurance policies. L&H insurance policies, on the other hand, also include disability, long-term care, and technical coverage (e.g., cancer, etc.).

Proper Insurance Provides Protection That Nothing Else Can

Insurance is an important aspect of a comprehensive financial plan because it protects what you have worked hard to build throughout your life. Insurance serves to protect individuals and companies from catastrophic loss—that is, an unforeseen event causing great harm that results in unexpected bills or loss in present or future income.

There is an insurance policy available for almost anything. Did you know you can purchase an alien abduction policy[1] for the "low" cost of $150 per year? The policyholder would

---

1 https://www.geico.com/more/saving/insurance-101/unusual-insurance-policies/

receive $1,000,000 worth of coverage against otherworldly abduction. Needless to say, this policy has never been paid out. Instead of focusing on out-of-this-world possibilities, however, your personal insurance program should provide protection against the kind of extreme, catastrophic losses that *do* occur in modern life.

To help clarify how to judge insurable risks, look at a matrix comparing *frequency* of loss to *severity* of loss.

INSURANCE MATRIX

Frequency of Loss Event		Severity of Loss Event	
		Low	High
	High	**Reduce Risk** (Change Behavior)	**Avoid Risk** (Avoidance)
	Low	**Retain Risk** (Emergency Funds)	**Transfer Risk** (Insurance)

- **High Severity/High Frequency:** *Any risk in this category is best avoided.* An example: extreme free-form mountain climbing. Since both the severity and frequency of loss (i.e., death) are high, insurance companies are unlikely to "buy" the risk from you. And in the rare case where an insurer will extend a policy, the premiums will be so high as to make the coverage essentially worthless. The extreme mountain climber who is worried about risk is better off avoiding the activity altogether.

- **High Severity/Low Frequency:** These are the types of risks that insurance is most effective against, and the kind for which insurance adds real value to a comprehensive financial plan. An example of this type of situation is being at fault in a car wreck and getting sued for damages. These infrequent situations are severe enough to set anyone's wealth building on its heels. Since the probability of loss is usually low, then the cost to insure against that risk is a fraction of the cost of the possible catastrophic outcome—but then, catastrophic events do occur.

- **Low Severity/High Frequency:** For a high-frequency risk, the transaction costs for the insurance company are also going to be high. High-frequency risk means the insurance company will have to pay a large number of claims, making it more expensive for insurers to do business given the personnel and administrative costs associated with each beneficiary. Think about how often your car gets dinged in a parking lot. The severity is low, but frequency is high. Since the loss is not economical to insure, it is best to reduce the risk as much as possible by changing behavior and parking away from the crowd or next to curbs. The additional benefits for a Henry are more steps for your health and less stress in vying for the closest parking spot.

- **Low Severity/Low Frequency:** In this the scenario it is best to retain the risk yourself, and be ready to address any needs through your emergency funds. For example, consider Christmas lights each year. You pull out the holiday decorations and begin testing strings of lights. Once in a while you will find a set that does not light. Instead of paying extra for the warranty coverage, you purchase a new set, since they are not that expensive. *Remember, an insurance company (or warranty company in this example) has to charge enough in premiums to cover claims, pay all its overhead, and generate a profit.* If the severity and frequency of the loss is low, then just retain the risk and keep the money that you would have paid the insurance company.

The italicized sentence above is key to understanding how insurance works and when it makes sense to include it as part of a comprehensive financial plan. In every type of insurance, the insurer charges more than what would seem commensurate with your actual likelihood of needing the insurance because they have to cover costs above and beyond the loss. When evaluating whether insurance is needed, consider how not having the insurance would affect you in a worst-case scenario. If the loss is absorbable without hindering financial security or affecting your standard of living, do not transfer the risk to the insurer. Only transfer catastrophic risk you cannot absorb.

Deductibles

A deductible is the amount of loss the insured must pay before the insurance company pays. For example, common auto insurance deductibles are $250 and $1,000. The difference in the two deductibles is $750, which is the amount of risk the insured either retains (with a $1,000 deductible) or transfers (with a $250 deductible). For someone truly implementing the Wealth Builder Challenge, the $750 difference in deductibles should be easily absorbable by emergency funds, which places this type of loss in the "low severity" category. (It is important to note that you need to have enough emergency funds to easily cover any and all deductibles you may incur.)

The premium on the $250 deductible policy is going to be higher because the insurer is taking on more risk. Our Wealth Builder, Henry, used to have a $250 deductible on his auto policy . . . until one day his personal financial planning advisor asked him about his coverage. When the advisor explained the idea of retaining low-impact risks and putting the extra money in his *directed savings*, Henry began thinking of all the things he could do with the money he would save with the reduced insurance coverage. He immediately changed his auto coverage to a $1,000 deductible and now moves the premium savings (which can be around $175 per year) to his investment program every time he renews his policy. Henry invests the savings of $175/year over thirty years, and assuming an 8 percent return, his account would be worth $21,411 even though he only "saved" $5,250 worth of premiums.

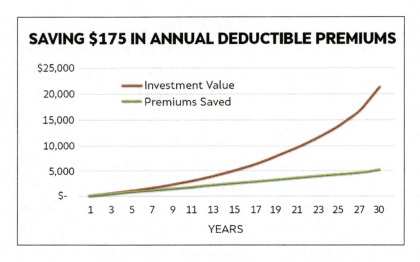

When Henry purchased his new television and was asked if he wanted to purchase an extended warranty (a form of insurance), he immediately recognized the low impact of a television malfunction and all the expenses built into the warranty. His advisor also told him that many credit cards automatically offer extended warranties on products free of charge! The money Henry is saving by moving his policies to higher deductibles and by declining to purchase high-cost, low-reward policies and warranties is going straight into his investment plan to provide long-term financial security for him and his family.

Liability and Policy Limits

Liability limits are the amount of coverage an insurance policy provides homeowners, vehicle owners, business proprietors, and others to protect policyholders from lawsuits.

The liability and property damage limits are what protect you from a high impact, catastrophic loss; the higher the liability limits on your policy, the better.

Auto Insurance

For auto insurance, we believe the minimum coverage should be $100,000/$300,000/$100,000, but $250,000/$500,000/$250,000 or $500,000 combined single limit is even better. This liability coverage protects you financially in the event you are deemed at fault in an accident and there are injuries and property damage. The first figure represents how much coverage the policy will provide to pay for the other person's medical expenses, lost wages, and potentially your attorney's fees in the event of a lawsuit. The second figure is the maximum coverage you have for medical expenses and lost wages to a group of people involved in an accident. The last figure refers to the coverage you would have to pay for property damage.

Homeowner's Insurance

As we illustrated in the deductible discussion, one way to keep the cost of homeowner's insurance lower is to take a higher deductible. Deductibles have moved over the years from a dollar amount to a percentage of the home's value. For example, a common homeowner's deductible is 1 percent. If the home is insured for $200,000 and a hail storm destroys your roof, your deductible is $2,000.

Henry understands this, and because he wants to keep insurance costs as low as possible without sacrificing coverage for a large loss, his deductible is 2 percent. He then accounts for the $4,000 deductible in his emergency fund. What does Henry do with the couple of hundred dollars he saves by moving to a 2 percent deductible? He invests it, just as he did with the auto premium savings.

Homeowner's insurance will also provide you with liability protection in the event someone gets hurt on your property. The injury may result from tripping on landscaping edging, or even a dog bite. When you complete a homeowner's application, the insurer will ask you a series of questions to determine the risk associated with providing you insurance; for example, they will ask if you own a dog, and if so, what breed. Your answers to these questions may affect your premium. We recommend a good talk with your agent about the minimum amount for your purposes, along with a discussion about adding a personal umbrella policy.

Everyone's circumstances are different, so have an open conversation with your agent about your risk exposures; for example, an often overlooked feature of a homeowner's insurance policy is the ability to extend coverage for jewelry. Homeowner's policies usually only cover $1,500 to $2,000 worth of jewelry, but you can purchase a rider, or endorsement, for additional coverage. Riders like this can be purchased for high-value items like diamond rings, musical instruments, and office equipment at home.

Umbrella Policies

After obtaining high coverage limits on auto and homeowner's coverage, it is usually best to purchase an umbrella policy to provide additional protection against possible lawsuits. An umbrella policy adds a million dollars or more of additional protection, and is actually quite affordable once you have auto and home insurance policies with high liability limits. Be sure to talk to your property and casualty agent to determine if an umbrella policy is right for you.

Life Insurance

It is human nature to avoid thinking about death, particularly our own death or the deaths of the ones we love. Think about your family and everything for which they depend on you. Do you bring home an income to pay household expenses? Do you have children you take to school, sporting events, concerts, or birthday parties? Do you clean house or make dinner? Now imagine one day you are gone from your family's life. The income to pay bills and the helping hand you provide disappear in an instant. How does your family's life look now? Will they receive a love letter, or will they be forced to sell the home, pull the kids from their current school, and be left to wonder about their future?

How Much Life Insurance Is Enough?

The best way to determine how much life insurance a Wealth Builder needs is to first develop a comprehensive financial plan, including retirement projections. This plan, properly prepared, will lay out how much money you needs to fund your current lifestyle up until retirement, and how much pre-retirement savings you need to support the lifestyle you desire after retirement. In the case of untimely death, most Wealth Builders want their families to continue implementing that plan in order for them to remain financially secure. With the knowledge of how much money is needed, a personal financial planning advisor can then calculate how much life insurance protection to buy.

One way to calculate the amount of life insurance a person needs is to conduct a Human Life Value analysis. Traditional Human Life Value attempts to replace all the future income of the insured; however, a good idea is only to insure for the amount needed to successfully meet your financial plan's goals.

What Type of Life Insurance Should I Purchase?

There are two primary types of life insurance: term and permanent. Each provides a specific set of benefits, some of which may be better suited to your unique situation than others. For a better grasp of the differences between the two, read on:

Insurance—Protecting Yourself and Your Financial Plan

I. *Term Life Insurance*

Term life insurance is a form of insurance that provides a financial payout in the event of death in exchange for a level or constant premium. It is called "term" because the premium stays the same over a specified time period, or term. After this term expires, the insurance can be kept in force, but the premium skyrockets. The best-laid term insurance plans allow for a low and level premium to be paid while insurance is needed. Typically, this would be your income-earning years. At the end of this term, the policy has served its purpose, and by following the Wealth Builder Challenge, you should have accumulated enough funds to take care of yourself and family, regardless of whether you live or suffer a premature death.

Term insurance is often referred to as "pure" life insurance because it does not build up cash value. When you pay the premium for term life insurance coverage, you are paying for death protection for a specified term and nothing more. Because of this, term insurance is much less expensive than permanent life insurance from the start. Because the life insurance company actuarially understands that in all likelihood the policy will not remain in force after the term period is complete, it can further reduce the premium costs. Term life insurance policies seldom pay a death benefit because they are typically purchased only by healthy pre-retirees to provide protection for their families while they are earning income.

II. Permanent Life Insurance

Permanent life insurance is designed to provide death protection for as long as the insured is alive. Permanent life insurance is much more expensive because the policy is actually designed to pay out a death benefit at some point when the insured inevitably dies; insurers have to increase premiums to pay those claims. Whereas the chance of the insurance company paying a term life insurance death claim is small, the likelihood of paying permanent life insurance death claims is much higher, if not certain. Additionally, almost all variations of permanent life insurance have a cash value associated with them. To oversimplify, this value is the difference in the premium paid on the policy and what the life insurance company is charging for the death benefit and expenses. The premium paid above and beyond the cost of insurance and expenses goes into the policy's cash value.

There are several types of permanent life insurance, and they all function differently. But there is a simple reason why it is not important to discuss those differences here: the Wealth Builder normally buys term life insurance instead of permanent life insurance and invests the difference. By using the premium saved and buying term instead of permanent life insurance to increase *directed savings*, the Wealth Builder takes another step toward lasting financial security.

There are times when permanent life insurance fits into a comprehensive financial plan, but without creating the plan, how does one know? Unfortunately, most people who purchase permanent life insurance do so at a life insurance salesman's urging. We generally find a comprehensive financial plan is absent regarding the customer's broader financial picture, unless it is designed to sell more life insurance.

Buy Life Insurance Sooner Rather Than Later

One important reason to purchase life insurance now is to protect your insurability. Life insurers perform a review of applications called "underwriting." Essentially, the purpose of underwriting is to make sure the insurance company is charging the correct amount for the insurance. By reviewing the health condition and longevity markers of the applicant, underwriters make a nuanced calculation of what policy will be profitable for the company. Someone in great health will pay less than someone who has a host of health issues.

Obtaining life insurance while you are younger and healthier allows you to protect your insurability against the possibility of an unexpected health condition. As people age, their health declines. The reality of waiting until you are older to purchase life insurance is that it is possible to wait too long. All it takes to become uninsurable to an underwriter is one significant medical condition. By purchasing life insurance sooner rather than later, you can have death protection while you secure your insurability. Unfortunately, many people do not think to purchase life insurance until they have a critical need—and by then, it is too late or too costly.

Disability Insurance

For the vast majority of working-age Americans, the ability to earn income is their most valuable asset. Income supports one's lifestyle and needs and provides retirement money. The Social Security Administration warns that over 25 percent of today's twenty-year-olds will face disability before reaching age sixty-seven.[2] This means the average American is more likely to become disabled at some point during his or her working years than to die prematurely.

What Is a Disability?

As with any contract or written agreement, it is essential to understand the terms of disability insurance. When it comes to long-term disability insurance, the insured must consider the policy's *definition of disability*. For coverage purposes, most policies define disability as either "own occupation," "any occupation," or some combination of the two. An "own occupation" policy is a good choice because the policy pays benefits as long as you cannot perform work in your current occupation. "Any occupation" policies can discontinue disability payments if you can work in any occupation.

Types of Disability Insurance

There are two primary types of disability insurance: short-term disability and long-term disability. Short-term

---

2 Social Security Administration, Disability Benefits, November 12, 2015, https://www.socialsecurity.gov/pubs/EN-05-10029.pdf

disability insurance typically begins paying benefits after the insured is disabled and out of work for seven days—the "elimination period"—and then only continues to pay benefits for three to six months. Short-term payments, hence short-term disability.

Long term disability insurance, on the other hand, usually starts paying benefits after a three- to six-month elimination period, and then pays benefits for a predetermined amount of time. Long-term disability insurance is usually purchased to pay all the way to age sixty-seven, but can be purchased for periods as short as two years.

If you look closely at the description of each kind of disability insurance, you will see they both have *elimination periods* before they pay benefits. The elimination period serves the same function in a disability policy that a deductible serves in a home or auto policy: to increase or decrease the amount of risk transferred to an insurer. The shorter the elimination period, the more risk the insurer takes on. Conversely, the longer the elimination period, the smaller the risk for the insurer.

Insurance companies know that many disabilities last a matter of months, not years, and if they use elimination periods to keep from covering these temporary disabilities, it reduces their costs. As with deductibles, the more risk you retain by choosing a longer elimination period, the more affordable the disability insurance. Remember the optimal

Wealth Builder approach: retain what risk you can cover with your emergency fund, and insure against the catastrophic risk of a lifelong disability.

Group Disability Insurance Policies

Today, the majority of disability insurance policies are group policies arranged by an employer or other organization to cover its employees or members. Group plans have guaranteed coverage periods during which new employees or members can accept coverage under the plan without providing any evidence of medical condition—that is, without having to go through the underwriting process. Though there are a host of other considerations when evaluating group versus individual disability insurance, that is not what this book is about. Simply put, individual disability insurance is better for the Wealth Builder to have, but since most people do not purchase expensive individual policies, the Wealth Builder should at least sign up for the employee sponsored group disability coverage.

Wealth Builder Challenge Takeaways

- Insurance is best used to protect against the catastrophic, so only look to insure against events that occur infrequently but are likely to be severe enough to affect your financial security.

- Consider higher deductibles and invest the difference.

Insurance—Protecting Yourself and Your Financial Plan

- Ensure that the liability coverage limit on your property insurance is high.

- Use "pure" or low-cost term life insurance policies to provide protection in the event of premature death. Invest the difference.

- Disability can be worse than death, and disability insurance coverage is a must. The best policies ensure that you are able to continue working in your "own occupation," and are payable until age sixty-seven.

CHAPTER 8

EMPLOYEE BENEFITS AND THEIR EFFECT ON TAXES

Employee benefits is an area that is ripe with advantage and controllable choices. And a financial planner can help you ferret out the employee benefits that put money in your pocket simply by knowing what to do and signing up.

We once had a client named Jacob who decided to leave public school teaching and start a new career in business. Jacob is young, ambitious, and married with two children. He came to us and said, "I am changing careers, and my new company is known to have good benefits. Will you help me work through my employee benefit package and see if there's anything I need to do?"

"Of course," we replied. "Send your package over and we will evaluate your benefits in light of your financial plan." After a thorough evaluation we were able to save or gain for Jacob an additional $1,200 a year by capitalizing on his HSA, employee stock purchase plan, and healthy living bonus. Do the math: $1,200 a year over twenty years at a hypothetical 6 percent is over $44,000 of value created simply by understanding what benefits best applied to Jacob.

Don't Leave Money on the Table

Life is sometimes filled with low-hanging financial fruit just waiting for you to pluck; you just have to know where to look and when the fruit is ripe. The worlds of employee benefits and income tax planning are no exception to this rule. Unfortunately, both areas are expansive and complex, which makes them intimidating to the normal person who just wants to do the things in life they enjoy and not be bothered with the encyclopedic, byzantine details of their employee benefits package or tax strategies.

On the other hand, as your financial planners, we enjoy digging into and applying these strategies, which add up to real dollar return for our clients. For example, Tony, one of our Wealth Builder Challenge clients in the energy industry, just received a promotion. Tony told us that due to his pay grade and the raise that accompanied his new position, he would not be eligible to participate in his pretax 401(k). After analyzing his options, we directed him to contribute after-tax dollars with the intention of converting that amount annually to a Roth IRA, thus forever changing taxable dollars to tax-free income.

The topics of employee benefits and taxes are broad and deep. Employee benefits apply to you regardless of whether you work for an employer or are self-employed, and taxes affect everything connected with Wealth Building. Since these topics are broad, however, we can only touch on some of them in this book.

Corporate Employee Benefits

When people think employee benefits, health insurance and 401(k) plans are usually the first things that come to mind. Health insurance and retirement plans are often the most expensive benefits provided by an employer, but they are far from the only benefits of value. We already discussed 401(k)s in chapter 3, so let's jump to other employee benefits now.

Health Insurance

Health insurance can be complicated, since many employers offer multiple plans from which employees can choose. Consistent with the principles we outlined in our discussion of insurance in chapter 7, we guide our clients to choose a higher deductible, lower premium plan known as a High Deductible Healthcare Plan (HDHP). These plans require policyholders to pay initial medical expenses of up to several thousand dollars out of pocket, but over time they are typically better than paying the higher premium associated with a lower deductible. On top of that, due to annual out-of-pocket maximums on both HDHPs and low-deductible plans, you are protected from catastrophic medical bills. In the scenario in which you hit your annual out-of-pocket maximum, that is when you fall back on your emergency fund or a Health Savings Account (HSA) if you elected to set one up. Those who are eligible can take charge of their health care by enrolling in the high deductible plan in concert with a HSA.

To encourage employees to participate in HDHPs, many employers will make a contribution to an HSA for the employee or offer a match if the employee puts money in first. The HSA contributions can help offset medical expenses below the maximum out-of-pocket, further improving the money-saving capability of an HDHP.

Now, to determine whether a low deductible plan or an HDHP is more likely to benefit you, consider these six factors:

1. You need to have an idea of how much in *medical expenses* you typically pay each year.
2. Determine the difference in *annual premiums* between an HDHP and a low-deductible plan.
3. Determine if the plans include an *employer-provided contribution* to an HSA or other health reimbursement arrangement (HRA).

4. Find out the *deductibles* in each plan.
5. Evaluate what the terms are for *coinsurance*. After the deductible is met, does the same coinsurance rate apply? Coinsurance is the amount the insurance will pay after the deductible is met. A common ratio is 80/20, which means that after the deductible is met, the insurance company will pay 80 percent of medical expenses and the policyholder will pay 20 percent until the out-of-pocket maximum is reached.
6. Learn what the *out-of-pocket maximum amounts* are for the plans.

Once you understand all these factors, take your expected medical expenses and run them through the assumptions based on an HDHC plan, then do this again for a lower deductible plan. After taking into account the difference in premiums and any potential funding of an HSA by your employer, decide which one best suits your healthcare needs and provides the most value.

It is also a good idea to run some alternative scenarios in which you have higher or lower medical expenses. Taken together, these steps will enable you to make an informed decision about which plan is most likely to benefit you and your family.

For example, below are projections for Henry's annual medical expenses:

HEALTH INSURANCE COMPARISON

HENRY'S AVERAGE ANNUAL MEDICAL EXPENSES: $5,500 (1)

Policy Feature	HDHP Details	HDHP Cost	Traditional Low-Deductible Plan Details	Traditional Low-Deductible Plan Cost
Premium (2)	$150 per biweekly paycheck	$ 3,900	$350 per biweekly paycheck	$ 9,100
Employer HSA Contribution (3)	$500	$ (500)	$0	$ -
Deductible (4)	$4,000 Meets deductible	$ 4,000	$500 Meets deductible	$ 500
Coinsurance (5)	25% $5,500 in expenses -$4,000 deductible = $1,500x25% coinsurance	$ 375	20% $5,500 in expenses -$500 deductible = $5,000x20% coinsurance	$ 1,000
Out-of-Pocket Max (6)	$8,000 Not reached	$ -	$2,500 Not reached	$ -
Total Cost		$ 7,775		$ 10,600

From the table in this scenario you can see that the HDHP saves Henry just under $3,000 over the traditional low-deductible plan. The plans differ significantly in that the HDHP shifts Henry's health care costs from a higher premium to the out-of-pocket expenses, which may be somewhat controllable.

It is worth pointing out how much it costs if Henry's family hits the out-of-pocket maximum. The HDHP cost $8,000 out-of-pocket max, plus $3,900 in premiums, for a total of $11,900. For the low-deductible plan, the maximum cost between premiums and out-of-pocket is $11,600. Our example is oversimplified because health insurance plans vary by employer, but you now know the importance of making an accurate comparison before you sign up.

Cafeteria Plans (IRS Section 125 Plan)

Many corporations use IRS Section 125 Plans, more commonly called Cafeteria Plans, which allow employees to use pretax dollars to purchase benefits. A Cafeteria Plan is a broad tax umbrella that allows employees to purchase health insurance, dental insurance, group life insurance, and group disability insurance with pretax dollars. Also, employees can often contribute pretax money to Medical and Dependent Care Flexible Savings Accounts and Health Savings Accounts. An employee who participates in several of these options can shelter a substantial amount of money from taxes.

HOW PAYROLL TAX DEDUCTION VARIES BASED ON EARNED INCOME			
2017 Wages	Social Security	Medicare	Total
Less than $127,200	6.20%	1.45%	7.65%
Greater than $127,200	0.00%	1.45%	1.45%

There is one additional and often overlooked benefit to Cafeteria Plans—the plans shelter the employee's hard-earned wages not only from federal income taxes (and some state income taxes), but also from payroll taxes! Payroll taxes are the levies the government assesses to earned income for Social Security and Medicare. As an employee you pay 6.2 percent of your wages to Social Security and 1.45 percent to Medicare, for a combined 7.65 percent. Social Security taxes are capped at $127,200 in earned income, so employees who make more than that will net a 6.2 percent deduction for the Social Security portion.

Flexible Spending Accounts (FSAs)

Flexible spending accounts are established under cafeteria plans and can be used to put aside pretax money for either medical expenses or dependent care expenses. There are actually two different FSAs most employees can participate in: Health Care FSAs and Dependent Care FSAs. Both types can be valuable to anyone who takes the time to properly use them.

Dependent Care FSAs are primarily used to pay for daycare or after-school care for children under the age of thirteen. The IRS limits Dependent Care FSA contributions to $5,000 per year.

Let us look at another example. Henry has a four-year-old son he takes to daycare every day; however, his employer offers a Dependent Care FSA to ease the financial burden on employees like Henry. The cost of daycare is $500 per month, or $6,000 per year, so Henry contributes the maximum $5,000 to the FSA. After Henry pays the invoice for daycare each month, he then submits that amount to the FSA administrator for reimbursement. Henry is in the 25 percent tax bracket and pays the 7.65 percent payroll tax on all his wages, so the $5,000 annual contribution to his Dependent Care FSA saves him $1,682.50 in taxes!

HENRY'S DEPENDENT CARE FSA TAX SAVINGS			
Tax Type	Tax Rate	FSA Contribution	Tax Savings
Social Security	7.20%	$ 5,000.00	$ 360.00
Medicare	1.45%	$ 5,000.00	$ 72.50
Income Tax	25.00%	$ 5,000.00	$1,250.00
		Total Savings	$1,682.50

A Health Care FSA provides the same pretax benefits as Dependent Care FSAs, but the IRS limits contributions to $2,500 per year. Health Care FSAs can be used for multiple expenses, including doctor and dentist visits, prescription medications, and contact lenses; notably, they cannot be used for over-the-counter medication or employer health insurance premiums.

Until 2015, Health Care FSAs were "use it or lose it" accounts, so all the money had to be spent each year. Today, FSAs can carry over up to $500 from one year to the next. Check with your employer to make sure their FSA allows for the carryover, because not all FSA plans allow it. It is also worth noting that Health Care FSAs cannot be used with a Health Savings Account unless a special Limited Purpose Health Care FSA is offered by the employer.

Health Savings Accounts (HSAs)

HSAs are only available to people who have high deductible health insurance plans (HDHP) that meet certain criteria. Money in an HSA can be kept indefinitely and actually invested in stocks for future growth. The amount of money one can contribute to an HSA varies by year and is dependent on whether the health insurance is for an individual or a family. If money is taken out of an HSA before the age of sixty-five and not used for qualified medical expenses, the IRS applies a 25 percent penalty on top of taxing the distribution as income.

HSAs are like a super Roth/traditional IRA combination, because if you use the money for qualified medical expenses there is no tax. Additionally, once you reach age sixty-five, you can pull the money out penalty-free and pay only ordinary income on the withdrawals that are not used for medical expenses. Contributions to an HSA are tax deductible like a traditional IRA, but withdrawals applied to qualified medical expenses are tax free like a Roth IRA. It is the best of both tools.

Let us go back to Henry. His HDHP premium runs $300 per month with a $13,000 deductible, and a plan with a $1,000 deductible runs $1,000 per month. He takes the $700 monthly savings and moves it to his HSA (subject to IRS limits) every single month. In about a year and a half, he has already saved $13,000, so he has the cash on hand if a large medical expense comes around, and he is continuing to build up his savings each month. If there are no significant medical expenses for several years, then he is way ahead.

Employee Benefits and Their Effect on Taxes

Employee Stock Purchase Plans (ESPPs)

Many publicly traded corporations allow employees to buy company stock at a discount of 10 percent to 15 percent. We generally encourage employees to avoid investing in company stock; not only due to the single-company stock risk, but because employees already have a significant investment in their employers—their paychecks!

On the other hand, certain circumstances can make an investment in the ESPP attractive. To be appealing, an ESPP should not have any holding period requirement after the stock is purchased. For many companies the employee can purchase company stock at a discount on a quarterly basis and then turn right around and sell the stock. For example, if an employee contributed $2,000 in a quarter and received a 15 percent discount, they would receive about $2,353 in company stock if the stock stayed flat. By immediately executing a sale, they would net an extra $353. The extra money is taxed as regular income, but just think of it as a company-provided raise or bonus! This strategy is as much an income strategy as an investment strategy.

Henry, constantly looking to build wealth, takes the extra $353 per quarter and invests in a diversified portfolio for thirty-five years at an 8 percent rate of return. The result? An extra $264,687 in his pocket from simply knowing how best to utilize one aspect of his employee benefits.

Often the hardest challenge associated with implementing the ESPP strategy is making do with a smaller paycheck. To make the most out of this employee benefit, it is best to contribute the maximum the plan will allow (provided there are no holding requirements), which results in a reduced paycheck—sometimes reduced by several hundred dollars. The best option is to transfer the same amount withheld for the ESPP from your savings to checking, so from a budget perspective you have the same income. After you sell the company stock each quarter, you can replenish the savings account and put the extra income from the ESPP toward your *directed savings*.

HOW TO MAX FUND ESPP AND MAINTAIN A BUDGET

Self-Employment Benefits

A self-employed individual can set up any of the corporate employee benefits we described above, but unless they are running a decent-size company, the costs to administer these programs outweigh the advantages provided by the benefits. However, there are affordable options with similar tax benefits:

Retirement Plans

If you are self-employed, you have several options for retirement plans in your business. Which plan is best will depend on how much you want to put into your personal retirement account, how many employees you have, your perspective on contributing to employee retirement accounts, the flexibility you desire, and what you are willing to spend on plan administration.

SEP (Simplified Employee Pension) IRAs are perhaps the simplest and most flexible retirement plans to administer. SEP plans are ideal for a sole proprietorship because they allow contributions of up to $54,000,[1] depending on business income. When employees are brought into the picture, though, SEP plans can quickly become expensive due to the contributions employers must make to employee accounts.

SIMPLE IRAs (Savings Incentive Match Plan for Employees) can be viewed as similar to 401(k)s, but are much easier to administer. While easier and less expensive to administer than a 401(k) plan, a SIMPLE IRA plan does not allow for as large a contribution as a 401(k). Also, once a business grows larger than a hundred employees, a SIMPLE plan must be abandoned for a different retirement plan.

---

1 2017 SEP IRA contribution limit. This figure changes periodically.

The biggest burden of a 401(k) plan if you are self-employed is the administrative hassle and required fiduciary duties. Typically a 401(k) plan will cost more to operate because several outside parties are needed for recordkeeping, administration, and investment selection if you want to discharge some of your fiduciary requirements. A 401(k) plan requires you to file a Form 5500 with the IRS, which often is done by the third-party administrator, and a fidelity bond also needs to be purchased to protect the assets of the 401(k).

In rare cases, a pension plan (technically called a Defined Benefit plan) can be a good retirement program for a small business. A pension plan is well suited to a small professional organization whose owner makes excellent income and wants to save a significant amount (more than $54,000 per year) to a retirement plan. A pension plan works best when the owner is older than the other employees. When it is appropriate, a pension plan can allow the business owner to contribute much more to the plan than other retirement plans would allow. To establish a pension plan, an actuary firm must be involved, so the administrative costs are higher than for all other retirement plans, but these costs can possibly be offset by the tax savings.

Other Considerations

Despite the freedom having your own business affords you, it is important to run it like a true business. What do we mean by that? We mean to operate your business in such a fashion that it has value to someone besides you. If you can build a business with value, then when you are ready to retire you can sell the business to supplement your retirement savings. Ask yourself, "Do I have a business with underlying value to someone else, or do I have a stream of income that does not exist without me?"

For someone to see value in purchasing your business, everything needs to be well run, with accurate accounting of true business expenses. Business owners most commonly go wrong by intermingling their personal and business expenses. Keep them separate!

It is also important to diversify away from your business. Many business owners reinvest in the business and spend everything else, leaving little for outside investments. If you do not accumulate outside assets it can become difficult to ever truly retire from or sell your business. In the book *The 10 Steps of Successful Small Business Owners: Your Roadmap for Joining The 2% Club,* Thomas Griffiths observes that small business owners are psychologically and emotionally tied to their businesses until they have enough outside assets to walk away. Once they become financially secure apart from their business, life becomes fun again.

Wealth Builder Challenge Takeaways

- Evaluate your health insurance options carefully and do not be afraid to choose a High Deductible Healthcare Plan (HDHP). Look for employer contributions or matches to an HSA or HRA.

- Use Cafeteria 125 plans to pay for as many employer-offered benefits as you can with pretax dollars.

- Estimate your medical and dependent care expenses and contribute to a Flexible Spending Account (FSA).

- If you have an HDHP, fund a Health Savings Account (HSA) on a regular basis. To jump-start your savings, use the difference in premiums between an HDHP and a lower deductible plan.

- Participate in ESPPs as long as there is not a holding requirement.

- SEP IRAs are excellent retirement-savings and tax-savings tools for the self-employed.

CHAPTER 9
MAKING TAXES WORK FOR YOU

As you know, the federal tax code is convoluted and changes constantly, but that can be a detriment or a benefit to you. It can hurt those who do not know how to minimize their taxes, but it can be beneficial to the Wealth Builder who understands how to manage his or her tax burden. Those who proactively manage their taxes usually fare far better than those who do not.

There are periods in a person's life when there may not be a lot of ways to reduce income taxes, but that can change as personal financial situations change. The key is to accept the necessity of paying income taxes, but keep a vigilant eye open for ways to reduce your tax burden when opportunities present themselves. In order to see and capitalize on an opportunity, you need to keep your financial plan up to date, and without the help a professional advisor holding you accountable, that is hard to do.

Income taxes affect all aspects of financial planning, from the types of accounts used to how to tap assets in retirement. Tax planning is important because it defies the standard risk and return relationship. There is no risk to legally saving on taxes, and the only investment required is a relationship with a knowledgeable professional. A dollar saved (in taxes) is a dollar earned!

Did you know there are 74,608 pages of tax code?[1] The tax code is very complex—more complex than it needs to be. In crafting a tax strategy, it is crucial that you work with a qualified tax accountant, but you will get even better results when you have a financial planner actively participating in the process. Here's why: Tax planning is the legal application of the law to reduce the amount of taxes you pay. The legal application of the law is not a loophole; it is the law. Therefore, it is our duty not only to minimize our tax liability, but also to apply the law through wise planning to maximize income and future financial growth. Why do Stans not capitalize on the tax law within the context of

---

[1] As reported by Wolters Kluwer, who publishes the *CCH Standard Federal Tax Reporter* for tax professionals, in their "2014 Whole Ball of Tax" summary. http://www.cch.com/wbot2014/WBOT-2014DigitalKit.pdf

their financial plans? Because Stans don't have a financial plan and they certainly do not hire experts to improve the odds of financial success.

Why the Marginal Tax Rate Matters

Another crucial distinction Wealth Builders need to be aware of is the difference between their marginal and average tax rates.

When it comes to taxes, most people tend to focus on the average rate because it is easy to understand how to calculate. The average tax rate looks at an individual's total tax liability divided by total income. You can look at your Form 1040—your tax return—and it is easy to see how much tax you paid and compare that with how much income you earned.

Wealth-builders, however, pay close attention to the marginal rate. The marginal tax rate is the rate at which each additional dollar the taxpayer earns is taxed. This figure is a more important indicator, because when we look at saving taxes, it is the marginal tax bracket that we measure the benefit from.

Here is a good example: Let's say we reduce your income by making a tax-deductible $5,000 contribution to a qualified retirement plan. Since the deduction is off the top of your income, the amount of the contribution would be subject to a higher tax rate, thus reducing your tax liability by more than what your average tax rate would be.

The bottom line is this: Most people have their eye on the average tax rate because it is easier to find, and perhaps more intuitive. But the marginal tax rate is what matters, because that is where the real opportunities lie for tax savings and growth.

Strategies for General Tax Planning

When it comes to tax planning, there are two broad categories: general tax planning and portfolio management. One of the big considerations under general tax planning is deciding whether it is more strategic to claim certain tax benefits today or defer them until a later date.

Let's look at the option of contributing to a traditional 401(k) versus a Roth 401(k). If you were to make a qualified contribution to a traditional 401(k), you'd get a tax deduction today. Depending on your situation, however, you might be better off contributing to a Roth 401(k), in which case you do not get the tax deduction today; however, you realize the benefit when you pull the funds out at retirement tax free.

There is a tradeoff. To determine the best course of action you have to know what is important to you. What do you value more? Do you value minimizing your tax liability today and receiving immediate benefits? Or is it more important to know that all the funds you pull out at retirement will be completely tax free?

This is one instance in which the marginal tax bracket comes into play. If you are presently in a relatively high tax bracket, then it is probably going to make sense to get the tax deduction today because you will more than likely be in a much lower tax bracket during retirement. Conversely, if you are in a lower tax bracket, or even in the midrange, the Roth option could be quite viable, as you plan for tax-free distributions in the future because you expect to be in a higher tax bracket than today.

Another key factor to consider in making this decision is age. The younger a person is, the more weight a Roth should have. But the higher the tax bracket, the more weight the traditional 401(k) should have. These types of choices also apply when deciding whether to contribute to a traditional IRA or a Roth IRA.

At the end of the day, it is simply a balancing act, and without the benefit of a financial plan, there is no clear-cut formula that says, "If you are beyond the age of thirty-eight and in a 28 percent tax bracket, this is the best course of action." Every circumstance is situational, like most financial and tax strategies.

Maximizing Your Roth IRA Benefits

Sometimes we get stuck in a particular mindset and become accustomed to thinking that things exist in fixed categories. But as you see, when trying to build wealth, you need to be aware of alternative pathways. A great example of what this means can be seen in the way we maximize Roth IRA benefits.

If you choose to go with the Roth IRA, you are paving the road to a tax-free future. However, there are instances in which, if you make too much money, you cannot get a tax deduction for contributing to a traditional IRA. At the time of this writing, the maximum contribution to an IRA is $5,500 if you are below the age of fifty.

Think about being faced with the following decision: Do I put money into a traditional IRA even though I can't get a tax deduction today because I am over the income limit? However, if I do make a deposit today to my traditional IRA, at least the growth will be tax-deferred and I won't have to pay taxes on the dividends, interest, or capital gains until I withdraw it.

But then there is the alternative approach, which is potentially more appealing. You can make a nondeductible contribution now, and at a later time convert that contribution to a Roth IRA. While there are income limitations on contributing to a Roth IRA, there are no such restrictions on converting a traditional IRA to a Roth. Now, this does not work in every instance, because there are some restrictions, but the bottom line is that by depositing nondeductible IRA contributions now and then later converting your traditional IRA to a Roth, you can work around the income limitations of the Roth IRA.

A Twist on the Conventional 401(k) Strategy

There is a similar strategy you can employ with 401(k)s. The IRS says that you can only contribute $18,000 each year to your 401(k) on a pretax basis. Now, let's say you are making good money and you want tax a deduction today. You set aside $18,000 as a pretax contribution and cut your tax bill for the year, which makes sense because you are in a pretty high tax bracket. Meanwhile, you still have discretionary income, and like most people, you are probably thinking about simply depositing to your after-tax portfolio. What many folks may not realize, however, is that the IRS sorts the 401(k) contributions in any give year into three buckets:

The first two buckets you are familiar with: your individual employee contribution to either the traditional or Roth 401(k)s, and the funds matched by your employer.

Many people are not aware of the third bucket, which is for after-tax contributions. It is specific to each company's 401(k) plan, but the IRS does allow for it. This means you can fill up all three buckets as long as you do not exceed the $54,000 max for 2017 (or $60,000 if you are over fifty).

This is a great benefit for the taxpayer who needs the tax deduction but does not qualify to make a Roth IRA contribution because they are in such a high tax bracket. They can instead funnel additional dollars above and beyond the $18,000 to their traditional 401(k) as an after-tax contribution. This is important, because although you will not receive a tax deduction for setting aside those funds, by doing so you open up the door to roll that after-tax amount over and out of the 401(k) directly into a Roth IRA, thus converting taxable growth to tax-free in the Roth.

Tax Considerations for Managing Your Portfolio

After-Tax Yields on Bonds

There are numerous tax considerations when looking at portfolio management, but we want to focus on three of them.

The first has to do with bonds. Stans tend to consider only interest rates when determining how to direct their bond investments. Neglecting to consider tax implications in your strategy, however, prevents you from seeing the full picture of that investment's potential.

When Henrys think about investing in bonds, they know they have a choice between municipal bonds—which are tax free—and corporate bonds or CDs, which are taxable. There is an after-tax yield calculation that enables the investor to choose the instrument that will be most beneficial to them.

Since most municipal bonds pay tax-free interest federally, it is more accurate to compare interest rates on muni bonds and corporate bonds with a formula to make it a level playing field on yield.

Here's an example: Say you fall into the 33 percent marginal tax bracket and can choose between a corporate bond yielding 4.5 percent and a tax-free municipal bond yielding 3.25 percent. On the surface, without crunching the numbers and understanding the different tax implications, a Stan would be inclined to choose the higher yield bond. But if you look at the after-tax yield—that is, the after-tax rate of return—you will find that the corporate bond yield is actually lower than the muni bond.

Here is the formula to find out the tax equivalent yield: 1.00 − 0.33 = 0.67 then 3.25/0.67 = 4.85% taxable equivalent yield.

$$\text{Tax Equivalent Yield} = \frac{\text{TaxFree Municipal Bond Yield}}{1 - \text{TaxRate}}$$

The lesson here is that you cannot exclude tax considerations when crafting your investment strategy. Doing so could lead to missed opportunities.

Tax Inefficiencies and Tax Loss Harvesting

A second tax consideration for portfolio management has to do with tax inefficiencies pertaining to certain investments. There are some investments (in particular mutual funds, but other stocks as well) that throughout the year spin off dividends accumulated from the underlying holdings. Some of these dividends are considered *qualified*. Qualified dividends are taxed at a more favorable rate than non-qualified dividends. If you want to be a Henry, structure your portfolios in a way that the predominance of distributions are taxed as qualified dividends.

Finally, let's talk about tax loss harvesting in regular after-tax brokerage accounts. Situations can arise in which given the conditions of the market at the time, you may have some holding of stocks, bonds, and mutual funds trading at a loss. In such instances, you can sell these assets, capture the loss, and use that loss to offset future gains.

If there are no gains to offset in that year, then you can use a portion of the losses to reduce your ordinary taxable income at $3,000 per year. You can only use $3,000 each year against ordinary income, but it is a good strategy to bank those losses and use them at a later time.

Additional Measures You Can Take: 529 Plans

If you have little ones at home, you might consider contributing to a 529 plan to save for their college educations. The benefit of a 529 plan is that the growth is tax-free, as long as the funds are used for college expenses. In Texas there is no state income tax, so there is no income tax benefit for contributing, but in many other states you can get a state tax deduction for contributing to these plans. You get the tax-free growth, but the 529 funds must be used at an accredited university or educational institution. If you have multiple children and one sibling receives a scholarship but otherwise does not use the funds, you can roll them over to another child or social security number.

There is a caveat to this mention of 529 plans: If you are on your way to financial security but have not yet achieved it, remember that your children can always get a loan for college, but you cannot get a loan for retirement. Your own financial wellbeing must come first.

Beyond that—and this is a hard thing to do—we encourage people to develop their own college funding philosophies. There are many approaches out there. Some parents plan to fully fund four years at a public or private university, which can get very pricey, whereas other parents want their children to have some skin in the game and pay for part of their education on their own.

Most people, however, fall somewhere in the middle. The risk of funding 529s to pay for all four years of college is that you are more likely to have funds left over in the accounts, depending on how many kids you have, what their academic ability is, and whether there will be scholarships available for them. This is not an optimal situation, because those funds could be put to better use in a different type of account—maybe even your own retirement.

Remember, this book is not meant to make decisions for you. Rather, we are here to share the wisdom gleaned from our experience, which we hope will stimulate your own thinking about wealth building.

Wealth Builder Challenge Takeaways

- The tax code is complex. You are best served working with an accountant and a financial planner to minimize taxes and maximize tax benefits.

- Do you want a tax deduction today for making a contribution to a retirement plan? Or do you want tax-free growth? You cannot have both, so it is important to know what you value more and why.

- You can funnel money into a Roth IRA other ways besides making a contribution, which can be limited by your income. Evaluate IRA conversions with non-deductible contributions and rolling after-tax contributions to a 401(k) over to a Roth.

- Be aware of tax opportunities in your investments: corporate (taxable) bonds vs. muni (tax-free) bonds, qualified vs. non-qualified dividends, and ability to harvest losses to offset gains and potentially your income.

- College savings 529 plans can provide tax-free growth similar to a Roth, but make sure you develop a college funding philosophy before the first dollar goes in.

CHAPTER 10
HOW FEAR CAN DERAIL YOU FROM YOUR PURSUIT OF WEALTH

Economic Nobel Prize winner and behavioral psychologist Daniel Kahneman wrote in his book *Thinking, Fast and Slow*[1] that we are actually hardwired to fear losses. This is something we cannot help. Therefore, we will do anything we can to avoid that emotional pain.

The subprime mortgage mess led to what we now call the Great Recession of 2008. Every time the stock market goes down into bear market territory (a decline of 20 percent or more), financial pundits seem to repeat the

---

[1] Daniel Kahneman, *Thinking, Fast and Slow* (New York: Farrar, Straus and Giroux, 2011).

phrase "It's different this time." Well, the Great Recession of 2008 *was* different. Never before had we seen major institutions like Bear Stearns, Lehman Brothers, General Motors, and Chrysler go bankrupt almost overnight. Equally unthinkable was that American institutions like Fannie Mae and Freddie Mac, privately traded companies that had the backing of the federal government, would be taken over by Washington. Many countries, including Iceland, Ireland, and Greece, among others, were brought to their knees.

Although the Great Recession was not quite ten years ago, some of our younger readers may not have been old enough at the time to truly appreciate how frightening a time it was. But Ricky Grunden, Sr. remembers vividly, so here we'll let him describe those days of palpable national anxiety in his own words:

"This time it really did seem different. I can remember lying in bed at night trying to connect the dots and predict what might happen next, which only led me to the realization that total collapse was a possibility. Frightening scenarios occurred to me: If the electrical grid would no longer supply electricity to my house, what would my family do? Modern homes are not built to function without electricity. For the first time in my professional life, I was contemplating the absolute worst-case scenario, and wondering what the strategy would be for my family and our clients if that occurred.

"At about that time, many others connected the dots in a different way, and determined that the only good option was to stockpile food, water, guns, ammo, generators, and the like. I had experienced that type of hysteria twenty-seven years earlier, back in 1980, when inflation rose over to 14 percent and gold hit a high of $850. (To put that in perspective, adjusted for 3 percent inflation, an ounce of gold would need to trade at $2,537 in today's dollars to equal $850 in 1980 dollars.) So I thought to myself, *What will happen if this all collapses?*

"Finally, I reasoned my way through my fears and came to the conclusion that enabled me to encourage our clients (and myself) to stay in the game: As long as we have rule of law and private property rights that are protected by the rule of law and strong enforcement by our government, people will still get up and go to work on Monday, regardless of the 'price value' of the stock market. There will still be major traffic jams on the highways around our metropolitan areas. I might have to cut back, but I will still buy food, gas, and utilities, and I will go to an occasional movie for entertainment, and billions of others will do the same thing across the globe. Slowly but surely, we will all pursue our enlightened self-interest and do what is necessary for our children and grandchildren. At some point, stocks will become so low in price that people with means will start buying them all over again. After all, given the rule of law and private property rights, what does a stock represent? A stock can represent valuable patents, real estate, machinery, intellectual property, processes and methods, . . . and good will. Some people at this time opted for real estate, thinking, *At least I have the land or the house.* But in reality, land and houses have to be backed by what? Rule of law, private property rights, and contracts—just the same as a stock!

"Now the thought process I just shared with you is logic—*reason*. People are not logical when they fear losing what they have worked hard for. As Dr. Kahneman discovered, people are hardwired to avoid loss, and when we become overwhelmed by fear and by our fight-or-flight instinct, we pull the trigger just to get relief from our anxiety. We must act to 'save' what we have."

Dimensional Fund Advisors in Austin, Texas, conducted a study[2] of net stock mutual fund redemptions on their own portfolio of mutual funds between the first quarter of 2008 and the fourth quarter of 2012, illustrating this point:

Many individuals and brokers panicked simultaneously, and fortunes were lost. Their "relief" locked in the loss and handed a big check to the willing buyers on the other side

---

[2] Dimensional's inflows based on their US-domiciled equity mutual funds. Dimensional estimated net flow data provided by Morningstar. Industry net new cash flow data provided by Investment Company Institute © based on the approximately 4,600 US-domiciled equity (domestic and international) mutual funds reported on an aggregate level to the Investment Company Institute ©. This includes information on Dimensional's US-domiciled funds during this period as well.

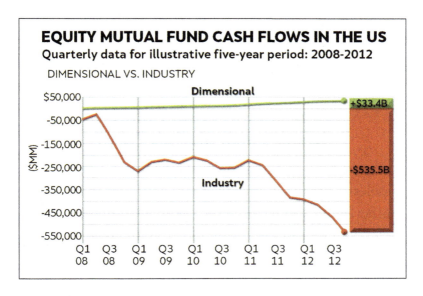

of the trade. On the other hand, investors armed with well-thought-out financial plans and advised by cooler-headed wealth managers (i.e., Henrys) held tight, and in some cases even continued to add to their portfolios while prices were low—as indicated by Dimensional's chart above.

Fear is a natural and sometimes healthy part of life. The problem arises when we allow fear to overtake our judgment and distract us from our long-term goals. When this happens, we make reactionary and irrational—that is, emotional—decisions.

Now what exactly does this mean? Just as those seductive photos of Stan's fancy boats and luxury holidays can goad us to overspend, the steady stream of negative news we are exposed to daily can cause us to focus on the negative at the expense of the big picture. At these times the best thing to do is keep calm and affirm that the financial plan you created when the waters were calm is the plan you stick to today.

Fear Factor: Losing Money in the Stock Market Part I

As we have already said, "Bad News Bears" can scare us senseless—literally. When we hear about riots in Europe or conflict in the Middle East or yet another corporate scandal, we lose our senses. We disconnect from the reason why we started investing in the first place.

Fear informs many of our decisions, and nowhere is this truer than in investing. Think about it: when you read headlines about the impending collapse of a foreign economy, or when you read that the Federal Reserve is going to raise interest rates, or that China has devalued their currency, or that the price of oil has dropped over 40 percent in the last year . . . how do these things make you feel?

If you are the average investor on the street, you might shrug your shoulders and go on about your day. If you are a stock trader, you might be tempted to sell the stocks you own in international markets or in oil. But the decision to sell those stocks is reactionary and irrational, primarily because most of the news you're trading on is already priced into the stock and bond market, and therefore it is too late.

How Fear Can Derail You from Your Pursuit of Wealth

Humans are hardwired for a fight-or-flight response when we experience fear. This often catapults us into investment flight mode: We do not want to endure the uncomfortable thought of losing money, so we try to escape it. By seeking to avoid the pain of loss, we become hostages to the myriad exit options available to us. In the process, we become overwhelmed. We lose balance.

One of the biggest challenges in succeeding financially is dealing with all the temptations that are thrown our way. There are countless products and services being offered, and a slew of messages floating around. There is a lot competition for the limited mental space of would-be investors.

We understand this dynamic quite well. In fact, a good advisor's job is to help clients fixate on their own paths and plans, in other words, to focus on what they can control and not on what they cannot control. There is a lot of noise out there, but Grunden works to filter it out and help you stick to your financial plan.

Let us acknowledge something else: Fear sells. As a matter of fact, it is perhaps the *greatest* sales tool. Sales people of all stripes know this, whether they are real estate brokers, politicians, advertisers, or news media executives.

The financial industry knows this as well. In fact, it profits from this fear. A key component of any sales pitch—whether it is an insurance agent selling "safe money" annuities or a broker selling stocks—is playing to fear. The narrative may go something like, "If you don't buy this annuity, you may lose money in the market," or "You need to invest in this stock immediately, or you will miss out on an opportunity."

Now, we are not saying there aren't honest, hardworking brokers and agents out there—absolutely there are. But it is important to recognize that many in the financial industry, like other industries, are in the business of selling fear to influence you to buy their product.

Fear Factor: Losing Money in the Stock Market Part II

These "bad news bears" also inspire investment-related questions from our clients. Our clients are no longer exposed to the kind of sales pitch described in the previous paragraph, but they are genuinely concerned about losing money based on what they have heard, especially when they hear of a supposed investment expert who is once again calling for investors to sell out based on their interpretation of the stock market. Instead of turning to sales pitches for expensive products, some clients will want to get out of the stock market completely, or drastically reduce their investment in stocks. The idea of taking such action is to try to be on the sidelines in cash, watching the carnage of a stock market decline, and then get back in and once they think stocks are about to go back up.

This idea sounds appealing, but in reality it is very hard to implement because investors and advisors who choose this route need to be right and lucky twice: they must make the right call on when to get out of the stock market (a decision that always looks easy in hindsight). Then, they need to make the right call on when to get back into the stock market, which is a much more difficult decision because now you have to put your money back into play with only an unknown future to guide you. Considering that no one can reliably predict the movements of the market for the next month or even the next year,[3] the odds of successfully making these calls are low . . . but that does not stop money managers and financial writers from claiming they can do it.

When we invest in the stock market, we invest for the good days. We do not know when they will come or how long they will last, but over time the stock market has gone up. If investors move in and out of the market, even infrequently, it increases the odds that they will miss really good investment days. In fact, just missing the best month out of each calendar year over the past ninety years would have resulted in dramatically lower returns than staying invested throughout the period. A dollar invested in the S&P 500 on January 1, 1926 would have grown to $6,030.71 by December 2016. If you had not been invested during the best

---

[3] For an intelligent and entertaining discussion of this issue, see Burton G. Malkiel, *A Random Walk Down Wall Street*.

month out of each calendar year, your one-dollar investment in 1926 would have grown only to $4.12 in that time.

The opportunity costs are even more dramatic with small company stocks. A dollar invested in the small company index of The Center for Research and Security Prices (CRSP 9-10) in 1926 would have grown to $33,816.51 by December 2016. If you had not been invested in the best month out of each calendar year, your one-dollar investment would not have grown at all—in fact, it would have dropped in value to just 15 cents.[4]

Henrys stay invested for the long term and do not try to time the market by moving in and out based on headline news. Henrys act on facts, research, and academic science to keep their emotions in control. Stans, on the other hand, are completely emotional and give in to every impulse to get out when the market goes down.

It is hard to prepare yourself emotionally to understand that when investing, a crisis is the worst moment to make a decision, because nearly all the information that is out there is already priced into the market. After all the sellers dry up, the crisis inevitably ends, and the market recovers.

---

[4] The S&P data are provided by Standard & Poor's Index Services Group. CRSP data provided by the Center for Research in Security Prices, University of Chicago. Both data sets were processed through the DFA Returns Program 2.0 twice—once with actual returns, and then again without the best month out of each calendar year.

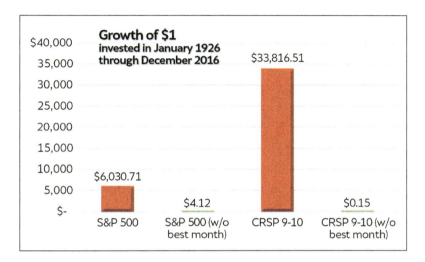

We have talked about the need for a written plan. The plans we write for our clients address their *need* to take risk, their *ability* to take risk, and their *willingness* to take risk.[5] Using these three metrics to measure personal risk tolerance allows Grunden to remove some of the fear from investing. Fear will always be lurking in the background, but the best way to combat it is with understanding and a financial plan.

If you do not remember anything else from this chapter, remember this: When you feel like selling stocks because of fear, you should *buy*, or at the very least do nothing and hold. The time to move is when you have a life change that

---

5 Larry Swedroe, *The Only Guide to a Winning Investment Strategy You'll Ever Need* (New York, NY: Truman Talley Books, 2005).

affects your financial plan. Though this is much easier said than done, following this one nugget of advice will enable you to avoid many poor outcomes and likely increase your long-term investment returns.

Plan, Commit, Execute

The Wealth Builder's Challenge presents a different systematic approach to accumulating wealth. This process emphasizes *your* values and *your* goals, builds an investment plan around *your* preferences and *your* temperament, and helps you overcome distractions and manage your fears and concerns.

Completely eliminating fear and emotion from our decision-making is impossible. Money management is largely an emotional event because money is attached to how we want to live. Regardless of how much money you make, it can be hard to stick to the plan of leading a balanced life *now* in order to have a better life later. However, maintaining balance is a commonsense strategy that enables us to weather all kinds of storms, and this is what Henrys do.

Wealth Builder Challenge Takeaways

- We are actually wired to fear losses. This is what catapults us into flight-or-fight mode: we do not want to endure the uncomfortable feeling of loss, so we try to avoid it.

- Fear sells, and it sells very well. There will always be "solutions" that purport to enable us to avoid loss, but these solutions can actually be a hindrance to building wealth.
- Focus on investing for the good days in the stock market. We do not know when they will come, but when they do come, gains are usually concentrated.
- To help combat the fear of losing money, create an investment plan to assess your *need* to take risk, your *ability* to take risk, and your *willingness* to take risk.
- Take the Wealth Builder Challenge to accelerate your wealth-building initiative.

CHAPTER 11
"I WISH I HAD MET YOU TWENTY YEARS AGO"

Whenever we go through our Wealth Builder Challenge process with a new client, after we develop and present the finished plan to them they are so thrilled to have the effective use of their financial resources aligned with their values and goals that some of them blurt out, "I wish I had met you twenty years ago!"

The problem with regret is there is no way to go back in time and change the choices you have freely made. Choices made over a lifetime lead to the life we live today. Choices, choices, choices, so many choices.

Many years ago a friend of ours told us something profound: "Everybody makes choices and then spends a lifetime serving those choices. Make wise choices, and your choices will spend a lifetime serving *you*." The reason we are writing this book is to help you repair the damage caused by the negative choices you may have already made, and to help you avoid the hardships that will inevitably come without a financial leadership guide like the Wealth Builder Challenge. And as another friend once said about making hard choices, "If you don't do these things, one day you're going to reach into your pockets, and where there should have been $100 bills, you're going to find dimes."

Our hope is that you will benefit from a professional relationship with a consultative advisor like those of Grunden Financial Advisory, Inc. Our years of experience will help you to steer clear of point-of-sale encounters and emotional decisions that can derail your potential financial success. "When you know, and you know you know, confidence replaces fear."[1] In short, you gain confidence and peace of mind. Our planning process enables you to make wise choices.

Most people are so focused on their careers and on becoming experts in their respective fields that they devote little time to their own personal financial planning. Think about it: How many years did it take you to attain the position you currently hold? What degrees and certifications have you earned? Just as with your field, learning to build wealth

---

[1] Don Boozer, Former Regional Director, Kentucky Central Life Insurance Company (circa 1980).

and ensure the financial security of one's family requires thousands of hours devoted to learning and research. To avoid costly mistakes and put the odds of success on your side, consider the value of having an experienced personal financial planning advisor.

A Paradigm Shift

One of the most important ways advisors can help build wealth is not by forecasting the stock market, but by getting to know and deeply understand their clients. While identifying, defining, and targeting goals is critical to success, it is equally important to understand why clients have those goals to begin with. To really grasp their motivation, we begin by engaging in a discovery process to understand our clients, their relationship to money, and what they want to accomplish in life. When someone meets with Grunden Financial Advisory, Inc. for the first time, it is only natural for them to have some preconceived ideas about what will take place. Maybe they are expecting a sales pitch. Maybe they expect to receive some complex formula that will spin their savings into gold. It may come as a surprise then, when instead of offering a menu of products and describing their merits, we greet them with a series of questions. For us, the first and most important step in the Wealth Builder Challenge is to understand the client and determine whether we play in the same sandbox. This cannot happen unless we ask the right questions, which is precisely what we seek to do in our comprehensive discovery process.

If this sounds at all familiar, it is because this process is our version of what a physician does. To safely and effectively treat a patient, it is not enough to prescribe a wonder drug or a complicated regimen. Whatever the symptoms, whether they are minor or serious, the first thing a physician does is take a complete medical history. Without knowing the patient, the doctor cannot treat him or her properly.

Values, Goals, and Relationships

Potential clients visiting for the first time are asked, "What is important to you about money?" This question almost always catches folks off guard because it is so unexpected. Most people end up saying something like, "Well, I can't say that I've thought about it all that much, but really I just don't want to run out of money." After a pause they may say, "I just want to make sure I have enough. I want my family to have enough money for . . ."

The way an individual completes that sentence speaks volumes about their values and their relationship with money. Their response may indicate that they are family stewards, ultimately concerned with taking care of their families. Or, if they are independents, they may say, "I just want enough money to do what I want to do—travel and enjoy life." From a simple little question, a door opens, leading to a wealth of knowledge about an individual.

Take Anna, for example: Anna is the sole caretaker for her ninety-three-year-old mother. When we sat down to talk about her future, she said, "Honestly, everything comes down to my mother. I have to be here for her." Of course this means not only being available to physically care for and emotionally support her mother, but also being financially able to cover her groceries, clothing, and medical expenses.

Once a person's underlying values are understood, the next step in the discovery process is to learn about their goals. When you start thinking about your goals in the context of financial planning, you may expect the line of questioning to go something like, "When do you want to buy a new car?" or "When do you want to retire?" But Grunden takes a different approach. In this portion of the discovery process, our inquiries are built around the question of "What do you want to achieve with your money?"

Personal goals have to do with more than the "when do you want to retire" question. Some people who are building wealth may not be able to answer that question, and even if they can answer it, they typically have no idea what retirement will look like. Financial security is often a personal goal, but it is funded by professional activities. Financial security can be misunderstood as having lots of money or retiring early, but what it really means is having the finances—and a plan—to fulfill both your personal and professional goals and being able to walk away from what you do today and move on to the next phase when you want to. Very few people can do that, and we want to add to that number for those who take the Wealth Builder Challenge.

Once the goals portion of the discovery process is completed, it is time to move on to the next level of understanding: relationships. How do you get to know a person and find out what is important to them? One way is to take a look at the important people in their lives; for example, consider the example above of Anna and her elderly mother. This portion of the discovery process delves rather deeply into the topic: Not only do we ask about family relationships—we even make inquiries into our clients' relationships with their pets! At first blush this may sound a bit silly, but for some people, pets are as important as children, especially if they do not have children of their own. We evaluate values and priorities beyond money; it's really about understanding the client holistically.

Assets

Having learned about a person's deep-seated values, goals, and significant relationships, next is the assets phase. This section is a bit more technical than the previous ones, since these questions invariably bring to light what an individual's wealth-building strategy is and how it came about.

We ask, "What is your current financial strategy?" In many instances the response goes something like, "Oh, I don't know. I just had to sign up for my 401(k)." Probing further, we ask, "What benefits do you get from the workplace?" We ask these questions in order to learn about all the options available to the individual from their company—if there is deferred compensation, more matching in the 401(k), or other benefits for the taking.

"How do you save or set aside money?" At this point many people look like deer stuck in headlights. One client, Sara, said, "I don't know, I just went to this broker, and she did it for me. She told me I had this much risk, and because of that I should buy this fund and that annuity—and that's what I did." This response is fairly common.

At that point we asked Sara, "How does this fit in with your goals and objectives?" After a long pause, she said, "Well, I never even thought about it like that. I just thought we were going to make money and it would be fine over time." Many people think this way, but to ensure this desired outcome, it is important to develop a well-conceived strategy—the nuts and bolts of which we explored in previous chapters—and to execute it successfully. This requires linking the plan back to the person, to their values and goals.

We have clients going as far back as 1987 who started out with less than $50,000 and are multimillionaires today. What common traits do they share? One key trait is that they have been successful in their chosen professions. Another is that they were able to stick to their plans over the years, adjusting those plans along the way as their family needs and goals evolved.

To address the topic of financial concerns, we first ask, "When you think about your finances, what are your three biggest worries?" This will elicit any number of responses, many of which are related to factors that are outside any individual's control—the uncertainty of the market, national debt, or government policies—but some of which will unmask problems with which we can help.

Then we ask, "What were your best and worst financial moves, and what happened?" A typical response goes as follows: "Well, I bought a piece of real estate—you know, real estate never goes down—but man, the property market crashed and we couldn't sell it. Finally we just had to unload the real estate due to a transfer for a better position with my company."

What we learn in this case is that the client has already had an experience with illiquid investments, which have promises of high returns but are not easy to sell in the event that things go south (and forget about making a profit). This memory, and the emotions associated with certain types of investments or risks, will have an impact on that individual's decisions and how they approach their investment strategy in the future.

By understanding what financial and emotional infrastructure is or is not already in place regarding asset management, we can better understand what additional scaffolding is needed for the construction of an individualized investment plan.

Wealth Management Consulting

As you progress toward your goals, your perspective on money changes. Instead of focusing on building wealth, you become more concerned with managing it. At $1 million of investable assets, we elevate our service to include the wealth management process.

At this threshold, you have probably mastered the six principles of wealth building and are now concerned about the management phase. We work with a network of experts to uphold the four pillars of our Wealth Management Consulting side: Wealth Enhancement, Wealth Transfer, Asset Protection, and Charitable Gifting. We work to understand how our clients approach each of these four aspects of wealth management before we educate them on strategies, services, and products. There are a host of different and more advanced planning strategies that come into play at this stage, but first you have to get there! It really is satisfying to see a client accomplish the Wealth Building Challenge and move into the Wealth Management Consulting phase.

Putting It All Together

It is important and enlightening for people to verbally express their values and goals so that they (and their advisors) can thoroughly understand them. Our approach to wealth building is not centered on secret stock tips, but on finding an approach that suits you. Arriving at that understanding entails a meticulous process of self-examination. This is where an expert advisor can assist, and where we at Grunden Financial Advisory, Inc. excel. An advisor's knowledge of global markets is certainly part of his or her value proposition, but it's more important that your advisor understands you and addresses the issues that are important to you. The important question is not only whether an advisor is "asking the right questions," but also whether you feel understood when you sit down on the same side of the table.

In Conclusion

It is the highest honor to be entrusted with our clients' finances, whether they are still building wealth or have already achieved their financial security. Grunden's Wealth Builder Challenge program is not for everyone: It is designed for people who are serious about building wealth and willing to follow our recommendations. Sometimes the marching orders will be hard—for example, telling a couple who are used to spending tens of thousands of dollars a month that they need to set up a budget and cut spending. At other times, implementing our suggestions will be fun, like giving a client a final stamp of approval to build that custom house because all their other goals are on track to be funded. Grunden's recommendations are based not just on a financial plan, but also on actually running different scenarios to see what is possible and what isn't.

Take the Next Step

As we said at the start of the book, there are no quick fixes or get-rich-quick schemes; anyone who will sell you such a gimmick is either deceitful or ignorant. The fact is, amassing a million dollars is a long process—at times exciting, at times scary, at times dull. But it is important to remain steadfast, to be unmoved by distractions or fears, and to keep your sights on what lies ahead—your secure future viewed through a financial plan.

There are a number of key steps in the Wealth Builder Challenge. We have taken the opportunity to outline them in this book, but the best results can only be achieved by a thorough consultation with one of our experts. To learn more, please visit www.WealthBuilderChallenge.com and contact us at info@grunden.com or (940.591.9007) to schedule a meeting (virtual or in person) with one of our advisors.

CPSIA information can be obtained
at www.ICGtesting.com
Printed in the USA
LVOW02*0105290617
539755LV00007B/494/P